WHERE WOULD

JESUS

LEAD

BOOKS BY GARY GOODELL

Permission Granted to Do Church Differently in the 21st Century

AVAILABLE FROM DESTINY IMAGE PUBLISHERS

WHERE WOULD

JESUS
LEAD

A *Study of*
CHAORDIC
LEADERSHIP

Gary Goodell

DESTINY IMAGE® PUBLISHERS, INC.
P.O. Box 310, Shippensburg, PA 17257-0310

"Speaking to the Purposes of God for This Generation and for the Generations to Come."

This book and all other Destiny Image, Revival Press, MercyPlace, Fresh Bread, Destiny Image Fiction, and Treasure House books are available at Christian bookstores and distributors worldwide.

For a U.S. bookstore nearest you, call 1-800-722-6774.
For more information on foreign distributors, call 717-532-3040.
Reach us on the Internet: www.destinyimage.com.

Trade Paper ISBN 13: 978-0-7684-3214-5
Hardcover ISBN 13: 978-0-7684-3389-0
Large Print ISBN 13: 978-0-7684-3390-6
Ebook ISBN 13: 978-0-7684-9126-5

For Worldwide Distribution, Printed in the U.S.A.

1 2 3 4 5 6 7 8 9 10 11 / 13 12 11 10 09

ACKNOWLEDGMENTS

My Friends Who Just Let Me Be With Them—I now have friends all over the world that simply let me be with them. What I mean by that is I don't have to perform, I don't have to produce, I don't even have to preach. I simply get to be with them as friends.

My Friends Who Help Me Think—One of these friends is Don Pickerill. Don got me thinking about church outside of the box way back in the 1980s, and I am still shaped by those early talks. My friend Doug Shearer, who stretches me and makes me think every time I read what he says, and the grace to let me say those same things again and again. My new friend Len Hjalmarson, who catapulted me into this project through his writings on "Leading From the Margins." My dear friend and co-author Graham Cooke, who makes me think about God like no one I know. And maybe even more importantly, he reminds me of how God thinks about me. And thanks to my late father, LaVern (Bill) Goodell, a great communicator and leader for 50 years, whose life reminds me how loving God influences others.

My Friends Who Help Me Write—A unique round of applause goes to my friend Rita O'Brien for her countless hours of work in helping to edit this manuscript. She does surgery on my run-on sentences and keeps me familiar with a special little punctuation mark called a comma.

My Kids and Grandkids Who Make Me Smile—The very thought of these people: my son Brian, my daughter Becky, their spouses Cynthia and Enrique, and those six littler people (my grandchildren): Victoria, Keaton, Maxwell, Savannah, Jackson, and Sofia—they all make me smile.

My Forever Friend, Mentor, and Wife of Forty Years—Janie

ENDORSEMENTS

"This book will stretch you! At least it does me. It takes me on a journey of what I really value most—love for God and people—and attempts to flesh it out in a real time setting. Gary Goodell marvelously and uncomfortably envisions the Body of Christ to be incarnational Christianity instead of ecclesiastical Christianity. True apostolic ministry is more about producing apostolic lifestyle and community versus just functional position. The content of this book is challenging and breathtaking at the same time. Someday I hope to live up to the security that is required to walk in leadership in such a manner. A new wineskin stretches as needed. Is your heart elastic? Read this book and find out!"

James W. Goll
Franklin, Tennessee
Encounters Network, Prayer Storm and Compassion Acts
Author of *The Seer, The Lost Art of Practicing His Presence, The Coming Prophetic Revolution,* and others

"Whenever I get to hang out with church leaders, one of my favorite questions to ask them is, "If someone were able to hang around you 24/7, would they want to be like you?" My friend Gary Goodell is one whom I know could answer this question in the affirmative, and that alone makes this book worth reading—he writes with the proven authority of a man who walks the talk. But there are other reasons as well. Gary's book blends a good understanding of biblical leadership with an equally good grasp of current church/secular culture. It also gives us a wealth of tested-by-experience practical wisdom and is written in an easy and genuine style. But it's the heart of the book (and the man who wrote it) that commends it to us more than anything else. Gary challenges us to reexamine our leadership in light of what Jesus modeled and taught. Where would Jesus lead, if He were leading today? I invite you to explore this question with an honest heart, with Gary as your guide. It is a journey that will change your life, and those around you as well."

Dr. Tom Wymore
Colorado Springs, Colorado
Simple Church Coach
Foursquare Denomination, USA

"This book is crucial for anyone who is currently going through the global 'shift' within the Church. To a man who is still in this process with a community of fellow-sojourners, this book comes as a cold drink on a hot summer day—refreshing. But it also comes like the surgeon's knife cutting deep into areas that need to be addressed: painful at first, but faithful. Let the truth in this book have its way with you as you read it. And may it help those who truly are seeking to be like Jesus in leadership come into that place with affirmation and empowerment. Thank you, Gary, for this book, for your years of friendship, and for 'getting out of the way' of so many like me!"

Tim Crozier
Encinitas, California
The Roots Church Network
Owner/Shaper—Blackbird Surfboards/King's Paddle Sports

"*Where Would Jesus Lead?* is a must read for every believer hungry for the reality of Christ. Walking with Jesus is first and foremost relational. Until the Church can model relational Christianity, we cannot expect the ever-present power of the "risen Christ" to be in manifestation. Gary Goodell points the path to the power—all we have to do is walk it!"

Al Houghton
Anaheim, California
Author of *Converts or Disciples, Marked Men, Purifying the Altar, The Sure Mercies of David, Jesus and Justice*

"This book is a plea to leaders, primarily pastors used to a classical church model. With authority, because of his own background and experience, Gary challenges us to embrace a non-hierarchical paradigm that will lead to effective mentoring of a new generation of leaders. We found the section on church gatherings especially helpful."

Tony and Felicity Dale
Dallas, Oregon
House 2 House Network
Authors of *Simply Church, The Rabbit and the Elephant: Why Small Is the New Big for Today's Church*

"*Where Would Jesus Lead?* will challenge, encourage, and motivate spiritual leaders to pursue a more authentic expression of the Gospel. I found myself affirmed as Gary Goodell addressed things I've believed for years but have not had the language for. I also felt very convicted as he addressed things I had overlooked: things that demand attention. This is a refreshing look at who we are and how we should live…no, how we *must* live."

Bill Johnson
Redding, California
Bethel Church
Author of *When Heaven Invades Earth,*
Face to Face With God, and others

"My personal testimony is two words: "Follow Me." *Where Would Jesus Lead?* helps outline "how to lead your followers." Gary Goodell does a wonderful job of showing leaders how to lead among the people by becoming a relational leader. A leader is to know those who they are leading. Gary helps define the leader's role as one who helps the followers develop and grow in their gifting. Jesus spent time with His disciples. He ate, fellowshipped, and even showed them how to prosper in their sphere of influence. Gary stresses the need for today's leaders to know and be willing to identify with those they are leading—as a shepherd knows and understands the life struggles of the flock. If you read this book, you learn more about how to lead those who have heard the call to follow."

Chuck D. Pierce
Denton, Texas
Global Spheres, Glory of Zion International
Harvest Watchman, Global Harvest
Author of *Redeeming the Time, Interpreting the Times, God's*
Unfolding Battle Plan, and others

CONTENTS

FOREWORD

Where Would Jesus Lead? is a book that will become a traveling companion for many leaders making the journey into a new place of Kingdom spirituality.

As we all grow up in our own place in the Father's heart and affection, we find ourselves at odds spiritually with our surroundings. To put it bluntly, we find ourselves occupying the middle ground between the Kingdom of Heaven and the world of the Church. Both places affect us differently. The Kingdom draws us into a dimension of worship, intimacy and embrace in the lovingkindness of God. Life becomes an encounter followed by a series of experiences that open us up into a place of limitless possibilities. By necessity, we must explore this clash of differentials or continually be disempowered by the system, which dominates in the Church.

The main change is in moving from a functional paradigm of spirituality to one where the accent is on relationships as a prime place of development for the presence of God. In effect, we are moving from a one-dimensional paradigm to a more powerful paradox.

Many of the theories and practices of the modern Church are derived from a functional paradigm that is more secular than spiritual. A paradigm is an approach to something based on an underlying assumption. In the case of the Church, that assumption is largely that people are sheep who need to be led, rather than people who need to be fathered. The leadership model is one of supervision, with departmental heads overseen by a management team presided over by a CEO-type figure. Vision, goals, and purpose flow top-down from a leadership that is relationally remote and task oriented. Of course, it is friendly and often kind (at least until it is crossed), but it has a strict order and its turf can be defended stoutly. The problem with this leadership paradigm is that it can never properly reflect God's heart or the Kingdom of Heaven.

In our relationship with the Father, we are children learning how to become sons. We are growing in our dependence on the Father and our interdependence on one another. We all have a personal calling and gifting that comes to us in our relationship with the Lord. This is confirmed by man but not controlled by him. The Church needs more fathers than teachers (see 1 Corinthians 4:14-16). Indeed, all apostles regarded themselves in a relational context of leadership with the people they represented. People were referred to as brothers, friends, and beloved children, sons in the faith.

What we are called into on a personal level with the Father must be ratified and become as deeply established in Church life. In a functional paradigm, it is often an individual relationship with

14

God that is overruled by a leadership insisting on their own version of divine order (see 1 Corinthians 14:40).

Changing from a paradigm to a paradox means that we get the best of both arrangements: relationship and true functionality (Mary and Martha). A paradox is two apparently conflicting ideas contained in the same truth. It is not either/or but becomes both/and in terms of principle and practice. In times of stress when these opposites are in necessary tension, the relationship is the preferred place in which to develop grace, love, and peace in the context of discipleship. We must be committed to making that change so that in God's eyes we are truly operating from a place that is decent, and in order with Heaven. The first area of difficulty that we face in this adjustment is that a paradox seems to be full of ambiguity and therefore absurd and illogical when compared with the rationale of a functional paradigm. It certainly requires a more heartfelt and considerate approach, which for a season will slow down the normal process and onward movement of the Church.

However, a functional paradigm by itself cannot touch Heaven. A Newtonian, mechanistic culture that values organization above organic life can never be wholly supernatural. It has no patience for mystery; no place for real faith, and ultimately cannot be fully led by the Spirit. Ironically, most evangelical churches have a leadership that has a structured spirituality, which is more pro-system than pro-life.

In this period of change, leadership has to be redeveloped so that it walks among people not in an artificial out/from style that is platform focused. It is a delight to work with such people who are having a fresh encounter with the heart of God and are therefore bringing their own life and walk with God into their leadership and ministry.

Gary's book allows us to explore that journey and gain an understanding of the terrain that lies ahead. He has walked off his map (Hebrews 11:8) so that we might have directions and a compass. Our place in the leadership of our work has become much more of a prophetic journey than we realize. "In me first" is a cry that should emanate from the hearts of all true leaders as we develop the capacity to be a catalyst for change and new growth.

The Church is moving from a purely functional paradigm to a relational one. At this time, it's an extreme swing of the pendulum that eventually will become a small series of swings between the two. We are all Marthas learning to be Marys also.

I believe this is a necessary leadership shift for the Church and leaders get to be the example that becomes an establishing of a new pattern/design of leadership. For the Church to step into its Kingdom destiny, how we produce people and develop them needs to be adjusted. We need people who are self-governed, innately powerful, with significant lifestyles in Christ, and inherently supernatural.

When we allow a relational paradigm to flourish and have precedence, then the way we function is radically altered. We simply cannot develop the relational and have business as usual in our functionality. It is a given, therefore, that our functional paradigm without the relational has developed some serious side effects that are not good for the current health of the Body and may impede its ability to grow and change.

There are many areas where a new dialogue can take place. A dialogue is not a discussion. That comes later. A discussion is a conversation we have when decisions must be made. If the need for decisions drives our conversations, then we never fully explore what is in front of us. We go only as far as our current need and thus effectively guarantee that our current mediocrity continues. Discussion without dialogue can only take us into a new place of measure. Same meat, different sauce. A dialogue allows us to explore everything that God has placed before us. Free from the tyranny of decision making, our hearts can go into places that our heads would deny us opportunity to explore. No idea is too silly, no thought too outrageous.

Someone somewhere thought of radio waves, microwaves, and infrawave technology—outrageous. Others thought of making moving pictures on a camera, in color (!) and then beaming them into every home on earth—ridiculous. All current inventions and upgrades were not born in committee rooms. They began life as a dream, progressed to a vision, and were built by relationships. What's true in the natural is also true by the Spirit.

A dialogue allows us to reframe our current thinking, abandon some perceptions, and adjust some principles in favor of values. We also get to ask better questions. If we are to travel this road, it is important that we see our church life in the context of story and journey. Everyone has a story of their own dreams and desires for relationship with the Lord and the pursuit of their personal calling. Our walk with God is the journey of life in the Spirit. Our collective story and journey is a significant metaphor for all that the Father is revealing to us.

> *By faith Abraham when he was called obeyed by going out to a place which he was to receive for an inheritance; and he went out, not knowing where he was going* (Hebrews 11:8).

He walked off his map. When the Lord does that, all our goals, planning, systems, and structures become secondary to the sensitivity of the Spirit that we are learning. It's a new order of life in the Spirit. The transition seems like chaos. Actually it is chaordic: A mixture of chaos and order reveals *chaord*.

Chaos is a formless matter, utter confusion; without order or arrangement according to the usual norm.

Chaordic is the behavior of any self-governing organism, organization, community, or system that harmoniously blends characteristics of order and chaos.

In a Kingdom context, it is the identity of the individual and the corporate man that harmoniously blends God's nature with the work of the ministry to produce a supernatural self-governing community that has power and purpose.

How do you move out when you don't know where you are going and God is committed to not telling you at this particular moment? Clearly having goals must give way to developing a sense of direction. We are learning about security through our developing sensitivity.

As Gary so eloquently writes:

It means leading by stepping off or away from those places of ecclesiastical indifference and entering into the context of someone else's life. Making a decision to no longer solely lead from one's age, one's stage, one's elevation, one's title, one's licensure or ordination, or one's tenure in the Church's hierarchical order. Central to this whole idea of chaordic leadership is the purposeful breaking down of many of those distinguishers of leader/follower, clergy/layman, superior/subordinate, and master/servant.

A relational paradigm is concerned with the fathering, relating with, and entering someone's experience—literally, the context of someone's life—and relating to people in a new mutual space.

This is really about leaders opening up their own lives and callings in order to relate to people differently. Normally, in a functional paradigm, leadership is friendly but distant—platform, title, status all diminish the space where people can connect with us successfully. Mutual space is where we share their journey and allow them to see, touch, and be a part of ours. Mostly it's more a blessed conversation that connects our stories.

In my home church, The Mission at Vacaville, we empower people to dream and give them permission to follow that dream. We tailor our training to the life that God is releasing. The vision of the house emerges through people's hearts and is not controlled through vision casting. It's mutual and owned by everyone. We prefer to teach people relational values and how to walk in trust, honor, and integrity. Therefore, we don't require control mechanisms. Leadership can become about something more than having followers.

The Godhead is a viable community of relationship and oneness of purpose and destiny within their mutual love of one another. The Church, made in God's image, must have the same dynamics at work if it is to be empowered from Heaven.

In a functional paradigm, man created the order (the vision) and asks God to bless it. We put the order before the people. If people do not fit our prescribed sense of how things should be, then we deem them out of order and place them out of fellowship. The idea that people can be "out of fellowship" in a functional paradigm is bizarre and ludicrous. The real (not new) order is about *agape* first and foremost. On earth as it is in Heaven. Love at the center of everything. Leadership is to be governed by agape, and the operation of church to be practiced in agape. Agape is who God is for us—unconditional love enshrined by an unchanging Nature that allows us to explore His heart and permissions.

The questions are going to come from a variety of sources as we travel this road. To be sure, they will arise out of discomfort, having our mind-sets challenged, the anger we feel at disruption, the learning we have to accommodate, the joy and wonder we experience, the freedom that provokes us, the behavioral situations we encounter, the permissions that are realized, the dreams that rise up.

Literally, all the questions have always been present but not able to be asked in a functional paradigm. Have no fear—they will all emerge as we journey and dialogue. A good question is designed to explore life and discover wonder.

This is the nature of apostolic leadership (not the modern CEO franchise apostolic farce we have today) and was modeled effectively by Paul. He avoided the typical hierarchical, externally imposed models of leadership in favor of promoting more of a self-organizing or self-governing way of community.

Here at Vacaville we have successfully abandoned the hierarchical model of leadership into more of a working/relational unity of team leadership. This has now changed again into a more synergistic style of mutual partnership. David Crone is still the team leader, but we have a very different approach to how we move the church forward.

I have been privileged to share part of Gary's journey into a more holistic corporate spirituality that is reaping dividends in the communities where Third Day expressions are located. I have experienced the favor of joining in with the dialogue that has taken place in the community of friends that is Third Day Church.

Leading with others as a team or staff has been acceptable modality and has worked for quite some time, even in the Emerging Church. Motivating ownership through team building works particularly well when a corporate image of the church must be maintained. However, when the Father introduces the same relationships that exist in the Godhead, within the context of the emergence of a visible Kingdom, then all that men have created as order must be redefined.

I have loved the dialogues that reflect our journey in the context of our responsibilities toward a functional paradigm whilst we are experiencing a relational one. We are learning to lead from among people not out/from community. All our leaders must, at some point, take the same journey. It's a leadership shift; otherwise authentic spiritual community is simply not possible. The structure will kill the life, when in fact it is designed to support the life. Any principle surrounding structure must give way to a value that says: friendship and flexibility over structures.

In a relational context, leading and following can actually be synergistically one and the same. Gary does it superbly here because he loves his personal journey, has no ego, and adores permission and discovery. I love his language in this book. Listen:

Classic leadership in the Church has always assumed that we are the leaders, the only leaders, and that the people are the followers. And, of course, we all know that followers must be led. We are taught that the masses of people in our organizations were born to follow. They cannot lead, they can only follow, they cannot feed, and they can only be fed.

Leading among is that art of being with others in that new, liminal "space," mainly through the one-on-one contexts and smaller organic relational groups, instead of defaulting to the old leadership model(s) that are based on leading from our assumed roles and anchored rules.

It's a very different lifestyle of leadership through relationship, friendship, and shared wisdom. Most church leadership is centered on efficiency and economics. How can we affect the largest number of people in the shortest amount of time with the least amount of resources?

The platform and position mentality puts a distance between leaders and followers and creates a status that actually empowers people in the sanctuary but not in life.

Chaordic leadership is about people. It involves coming alongside them for their personal growth, development, and maturity. It is concerned with their story, their journey, and their destiny.

Leadership is not only being redefined in a relational context, it is also being repositioned in a relational and functional paradox. For so long we have only had the functional paradigm to work in so we chose management; the creation of systems and structures; tasks and goals; economy and efficiency, which all required planning, strategy, and vision in order for a small group of leaders to take the mass of followers—somewhere.

Now, the Father is inviting leaders to come from behind a series of barricades (titles, status, position, "full time" leader, ministry) that have maintained an artificial distance and learn to walk among, alongside people in partnership. We are learning to lead by listening, learning, and laughing as we stroll with people and even follow their lead as they move into their rightful place in the Spirit.

The style, focus, and intentions are very different between a supernatural, relational community and distanced institutional leading.

Enjoy your own journey first. Come into the fullness of it. Learn the abundance that it facilitates in you. Celebrate who you are and what you are becoming.

Start a series of conversations with your current leaders about their journey. Who are they becoming? In this move of God toward absolute favor, what will change in them the most? How has the system and the structure imprisoned their heart? Are they leading as servants or sons?

Do you see the different questions that become possible? In transition, we often find ourselves seeking answers to questions that are no longer relevant.

This kind of relational life-commitment community has a hard time fitting in the promotion-oriented church leadership systems today.

Our first priority is to be rightly related to the Father and to join the Godhead in their approach to community. They are a community in themselves. The nature of God is a community of oneness. They function as a relational community in creation. In Genesis 1:1-3 we see the Father at work in creation (v. 1); the Spirit brooding over it (v. 2), and the Word (v. 3) being released into it.

Community is a way of being that enables and empowers people to walk as the Godhead walks—to be in a divine mode of being that is in line with God's own existence. God loves community because He continually experiences the dynamics and synergy of three in one. So, when He creates in His own image, He creates community.

God is a community of Father, Son, and Holy Spirit. Each an uncreated person, one in essence, equal in power and glory. That community runs on love, honor, and mutual interdependence with joy, peace, and a lasting commitment to relationship first.

I believe our responsibility lies not in maintaining a structure but in redefining the way that we want to walk in our own leadership team. Who and what do we want to become for them? We don't have to dismantle the structures, we only have to adjust them to fit the life that is growing in our midst. We can do that as we grow. The key proposition is: We are not seeking to maintain our functional paradigm and bolt relationships onto it. We are redefining what relationship, community, and friendship is and how we reposition our leadership to walk among people in order to listen, learn, facilitate, and enjoy what the Holy Spirit is doing among us. For God to walk among us, we must have a leadership made in the same image.

We should be concerned with vertical intimacy and horizontal influence. We facilitate people into a different place in the heart of

God so that they are discipled into relationship with the Father that affects their leadership and friendship with others.

This new relationship requires a new language; a fresh heart and a change of mind-set. It is also means a new oneness, a community within the leadership.

A new paradigm demands a new rhythm. A different way of being, and a more distinctive place of peace and rest in which to operate. Currently, our internal place of relationship can be threatened by the external requirements of the system we maintain to keep an order that is no longer relevant or required.

Being with the leadership and their journey is most vital. We can gradually let the system run down over time as we input new things that redefine our corporate journey. As things come to an end, we don't replace them with structures from the old model. We can safely outgrow some things. It's a relational transition, not a functional one. Vertical intimacy meets horizontal influence.

If we only think about changing the system and developing new structures, we are not operating relationally. Function still has the upper hand, and Mary is forced to help Martha. In a paradox, what has primacy when all is under pressure? Choose the good part—relationship and friendship, intimacy with God and one another.

Change is not about speed but rhythm. If we slow down relationally, we will do more functionally; but the timing will be different. In a functional paradigm, we are used to implementing new things that yield measurable results quickly. In a relational/ functional paradox, more growth occurs eventually. What we measure is the change in people. We measure their joy, peace, laughter, desire, passion, initiative, and personal sense of destiny, identity and persona.

It takes time for a big ship to turn. It took Vacaville around three years to move into a completely different style of community over church. Three to six years is the norm, unless the main leader has a personal encounter with God that changes his life.

Without encounter, there is no real change. We make adjustments, but the modality is essentially the same. It's the same meat, different sauce. How do we change from being purpose-driven to becoming presence-oriented in our relationships, not just our meetings?

Our rest and peace is our own responsibility. They are not driven by everything being OK in the church. Rest and peace are not circumstantial, but they do come into their power during a storm. They affect circumstances but are untouched by them.

Tension does not mean that something is wrong. It means something is happening. There is no movement without tension. We cannot get a grip on anything physically unless tension is present. We must ensure that tension does not become a friction. A relational paradigm chooses people, not systems. It is only slower initially, but it will gather pace exponentially, and we will have the joy of going in a different direction.

In a relational/functional paradox, we can encounter a divine acceleration. A momentum is possible when we really transition with faith and patience into the fullness that God has for us.

As we lead from among, we can listen for what God is saying in the people around us. I have no doubt that we are passing through territory where people want new but think old. When we don't know where we are going, how we travel is important.

Lead as a celebrant. A functional mind-set wants to know details so it can function, which is fair—except when we are changing a paradigm into a paradox. When we are changing purpose-driven into presence-oriented, the rules change. So do the rhythm, the energy, and the focus.

In relationship with God, we celebrate. He is full of joy. Rejoicing is our response to His joy. We bask in His peace. We walk in His love. We enjoy life and people. Vertical intimacy, horizontal influence.

There is a new language, new lifestyle, new mind-set, new timing, and a different rhythm we have to adjust to in the Spirit. There are new questions we should be asking. We are moving in a new direction; therefore, the Church cannot move in the same modality.

If (and He is!) the Lord is taking us on a new journey, then He must and will take responsibility for the welfare of the people travelling with us. We must focus on enjoying this new partnership with the Father and relaxing into Him especially in the role that He wants us to have.

Gary has been my friend for a number of years. We have loved, enjoyed, and mentored one another into a shared mutual space. Our expressions of church are very different but our values and principles are exactly the same. The Kingdom not only allows for such differences but also actively encourages them. Welcome to the beauty of the majesty that is the Nature of God; never a stereotype, always a prototype.

Reading this book will open you up to questions that will provoke a dialogue with the Lord and fellow travelers. Gary and I hope to see you on the journey some time!

Graham Cooke

Graham has written 16 books and co-authored 2 more, including *"Permission Granted to Do Church Differently in the 21st Century"* with Gary Goodell. He is a well-known conference speaker and functions as a consultant, helping churches make the transition from one dimension of calling to a higher level of vision and ministry.

INTRODUCTION TO CHAORDIC LEADERSHIP

THIS BOOK IS NOT MEANT TO FIT into today's classic leadership literature. It is not about addressing management strategies and numerical success. It is, in fact, more a map than a manual, more a sign than a seminar. Hopefully, it is part of the new GPS tracking system for navigating leadership development into the next generation.

This book is written to that specific generation of Christian leaders who have led predominantly from one sacred ecclesiastical space. That one spot, with its pulpits, its lecterns, its spotlight, its center stage. The proverbial holy man, leading the holy ritual, on the holy day, at a holy hour, from the holy place, and doing holy things for a holy fee.

These chapters propose a certain notion or idea that those of us who have practiced leading from one place and in one way, most of our lives, might be willing to find a new place and a new way to lead, which may, in fact, help better prepare the next generation of leaders for their next leg of their journey.

Having spent the bulk of our ministry careers leading from in front of a group, this is a challenge to step into an exotic environment that may not be quite as clean, quite as orderly, or quite as prestigious, and definitely not as safe as our old leadership slots.

It is an open invitation to lead among those we serve, not just in front of them—not from our positions or titles or roles, but actually among them.

Using organizational jargon, *chaordic* or *chaord* refers to the behavior of self-governing organisms, organizations, or systems. It means the art of being adaptive, often nonlinear, ebbing and flowing between the characteristics of order and chaos. Most of this basic definition is spelled out the best by the guru of chaordic leadership, Dee Hock in his landmark book, *"Birth of the Chaordic Age."*

From discipleship or leadership paradigms, it means leading by stepping off or away from those places of ecclesiastical indifference and entering into the context of someone else's life. Making a decision to no longer solely lead from one's age, one's stage, one's elevation, one's title, one's licensure or ordination, or one's tenure in the church's hierarchical order.

It means the act of stepping into someone else's "chaos" in order to model, bring guidance and hopefully to help bring or shape some "order." An act of leading in a "cha-order" way, a "chaordic way."

Introduction to Chaordic Leadership

Central to this whole idea of chaordic leadership is the purposeful breaking down of many of those distinguishers of leader/follower, clergy/layman, superior/subordinate, and master/servant. It requires a new order, a new way of seeing everything we have known organizationally. It will be collaborative, chaordic, an open social archtype or tribal prototype style of organizing and leading.

It will demand that leaders leave the world of the clergy executive elitism and enter someone else's experience, someone else's world, and it will demand a rare commitment to relate to people in their place, not ours.

This way of relating to others often alters the equilibrium of leaders by affecting the genesis of all leadership, namely the place or places from which leaders normally lead and often hide. It is this unique "special place" mentality that has often fed other artificial distinctions, creating a class system out of the family of God.

Many concepts and practices of chaordic or collaborative leadership are actually not new or revolutionary. Some believe that the apostle Paul himself used them in guiding such communities as the church at Corinth, as he actually avoided the typical hierarchical, externally imposed models of leadership in favor of promoting more of a self-organizing or self-governing way of community, what some modern scientists call the "chaos theory."

Although motivating a select chosen few as a leadership team or a staff has been an acceptable modality for leading within the corporate image of the church or organization must be maintained, to actually step away from the security of our "sacred place" and to distinctly lead with or among others still seems foreign.

But as the forces of globalization and technology are leveling traditional hierarchies, and even accepted norms of communication, chaordic leadership is critical to bringing a refreshing structural shift to the current practice of today's top-down clergy leadership.

As we all know, the massive impact of the current tools of social communication like Facebook, YouTube, and Wikipedia represent not only a shift in the way we access information, but how we understand authority.

In essence, these new social networks have "flattened the Church," removing many of those preconceived ideas about hierarchical roles and positions. Now, in a simple post on the Internet on a popular social network, all of the contributors are on the same level, on the same page, experiencing, bickering, battering, and exchanging the same input at the same time.

In the chaordic or collaborative leadership world, the idea is that leading and following can actually be synergistically one in the same.

Dee Hock shares,

In every moment of life, we are simultaneously leading and following. There is never a time when our knowledge, judgment and wisdom are not more useful and applicable than that of another. There is never a time when the knowledge, judgment and wisdom are not more useful and applicable than another.[1]

And while the Chaordic Age, as it has been called, has taken the corporate world by storm, the shift to chaordic leadership as a working model for discipleship and church leadership remains a huge stretch.

Overled and Overfed

Classic leadership in the Church has always assumed that we are the leaders, the only leaders, and that the people are the followers. And, of course, we all know that followers must be led. We are taught that the masses of people in our organizations were born to follow. They cannot lead, they can only follow, they cannot feed, and they can only be fed.

This mind-set is deeply instilled and assumed in all of the current leadership training. Built into this corporate church concept or system is the rule that the ordained clergy are the appointed leaders and that the parishioners (or laymen) are the followers. And please note that in today's clergy rule book, this is inferred as being God's actual matrix and must not be altered.

A deep systemic root that chaordic leadership confronts is the assumed permanent role that we are leaders all of the time in all of our relationships. And, of course, as we habitually minister from that assumption, we will keep overlooking the truths, missing the revelations, and even ignoring the fact that leadership also comes from others, and even from those we feel assigned to lead. It is hard to even begin to address these issues, when those lines between teacher/student roles continue to blur.

Whenever we discover that we are not the permanent leader all the time, a wonderful shift happens in our relationships. Because mutual mentoring thrives best through reciprocally open relationships, we can even start enjoying *not* leading and just being with those we are called to lead.

Of course, this shift can place great strain on long-term vocational ministers. At the very heart, it means that we must be willing to submit ourselves to those we live among and lead, rather than suggesting that their submission to us is of a much higher and more sacred order.

My generation of leaders was identified because of where we stood on the organizational chart, and what the nameplates on our office doors and our desks echoed. Ignoring these flow charts and name placards means that those who are not on the charts and those whose nametags are not printed may also be full of the same Holy Spirit and ready to rise to leadership.

This means that our followers really do not have a 30-day-trial Holy Spirit or a junior Holy Spirit, or even baby Christian Holy Spirit. It means that we will have to recognize their giftings and their wisdom and what they bring to the table, and invite and accept them as a great benefit to us.

We are up against some pretty stiff addictions to these old models from the "good old boys" when we begin to advocate new formats of leadership that threaten the status quo of how we have led for generations of the Church. And this can be an uphill climb when we understand that most of the dominant models of leadership come from the West, and generally from generations of Caucasian men.

Our current sacred grids for church leadership are some of the oldest, strongest, deepest, and most resistant to change. But, these changes are not optional if we are intent on involvement in cross-training leadership development for the future. We have no choice; the next level of church leadership requires it.

Liminal Leadership

This *leadershift* is a shift toward a strange and new place. It is a "chaordic place," or what some even call a *liminal space.*[2] *Liminality* is actually from the Latin word *limen*, meaning "a barely perceptible threshold," or a place in between two worlds, or a place of transition. The liminal state is characterized by ambiguity, openness, and indeterminacy, including the possibility that one's own sense of identity can dissolve to some extent, bringing about a very frightening disorientation.

Liminality is a period of transition where normal limits to thought, self-understanding, and behavior are relaxed—a situation that can lead to a whole new perspective.

In this "space" or "place," people, places, or things are in a state of transition between the possible and not yet fully realized. In entering into this place, get ready for "chaos" and "chaordic" moments.

In this mysterious place, this bridge place, one finds a unique balance between the people you are leading and the God you are both following. It is destined to be more of a prophetic place than a pastoral place, and definitely more of an obscure place than an obvious one.

In this place, you enter a strategic cooperation with what God is telling those you lead and what God is telling you. In this newly discovered tutoring place, we will operate as a guide and a coach, and a mysterious fellow traveler on the same journey but without becoming the focal point of the excursion. It is so mysterious, the Irish used to say, "It is the place between the foam and the sea."

And this place asks the big question: Is your leadership style all about you and your ministry and what you get from leading? Or is it about serving those you lead, helping to get them going on the God journey that they are destined to trek?

Generations of Leaders

The hunger most evident in this next generation is for fathers and mothers, and not a new BFF. They need fathers and mothers who will forgo their own controlling preoccupations with how things used to be done, giving space to their willingness to enter into the experiment, stepping off the map to go where God might lead the next generation.

A relationship is required, but a script is not. Times of resting, times waiting in prayer, and times of silence represent more of this new adventure than the exhausting attempts at preresearch to make sure every step is sure-footed. Like mountain goats, the instinct of where to step and where to go comes in the moment, and not the preplanned staff meetings. It is a journey with forward movement as its goal, and not just another stroll down memory lane where we remind our students of how it used to be done. And not just another dress rehearsal that ends in disappointment. We are actually going somewhere.

So, as this book will try to illustrate, we first find those we are called to lead in the next generation of leaders and begin by committing to not overlead or overfeed. This time we get into the journey with them and see how God will use us both along the trip.

He will use our tested experience and obedience, but as well will turn up the pace as He capitalizes on the speed of the younger leaders we are running with. It is a new pace, not tried; it is a new direction, not learned. And it is the excitement of a new adventure for both you and the one you will run with.

With this new basic metaphor describing and assessing Christian leadership as "spatial" or a *"space between,"* we must then make every effort to discover that "space." And then do whatever it takes to stay in that "space." Try not to retreat and return to the old default of what you tell others to do.

For those who think this is just another cheap shot at pastors, joining today's preoccupation with "church bashing," or "preacher picking," sorry, you're wrong. The challenge this book brings will only make you feel that way if your view of leadership is lectures, lectures, and more lectures, programs, programs, and more programs.

I am not one of those typical ersatz critics wanting to "throw the baby out with the bathwater," when it comes to leadership renewal and church reformation. I am a seasoned churchman and a committed advocate of change, especially when it comes to making a strategic attempt to step away from some of the norms and habits of the modern church system and culture. And I love experimenting with tried and true, verifiable methods for making more effective disciples more effectively.

This is about you finding your new *space between*. But be assured, this is a place that God has actually been wooing you to enter for a long time.

If you want to make radical, transformed disciples, and if you understand the basic laws of learning and pedagogy, or the way people learn, you must give way to more and more experiences of walking together with those you intend to lead and disciple.

Our old place required good speakers—this new one needs good listeners. The old one required preplanned handouts and formatted teaching outlines—this new one means serendipitous discussions and surprising interactions.

This new or fresh way of doing church and doing discipleship differently responds to the now common sentiments felt by many currently exiting the "cathegogue" (cathedral/synagogue) institutional footprint of weekend church in a search for something more organic, more authentic, and more relational. The picture here for your mind's eye is that of a couple of guys in animated discussion in the corner of the coffee shop, rather than the charismatic presentation to controlled parishioners.

Information Dispensers or Disciple Makers?

In our Information Age we have become like the old-fashioned Pez candy dispensers continuing to dispense endless packages or portions of information called sermons, hoping that these information transactions produce life, comfort, inspiration, and even discipleship.

But somewhere between our pulpits and the people, somewhere between the stage and the situation, we have been invited to move from a tradition functional leadership model and to not just find, but to actually occupy, a new place and a new space in someone else's life through an intentional incarnational model of leadership.

Chaordic leadership then becomes chaordic discipleship, something that all believers are called to do, whether it is discipling or training your children, coworkers, or the people in your fellowship that you feel assigned by God to walk among.

How will we ever get there? Hopefully, this book will help you to explore, examine, and experience that amazing journey.

Endnotes

1. Dee Hock, *Birth of the Chaordic Age* (San Francisco, CA: Berrett-Koehler Publishers, 1999), 72.

2. Alan Roxburgh, *The Sky is Falling* (Eagle, ID: ACI Publishing, 2005), 49.

CHAPTER 1

"Now, Heeere's, Johnny!"

I AM NOT IGNORING CHURCH HISTORY, nor missing the context and traditions of the American Church. And I do know that the bulk of the tooling and training for our Western pulpiteering model is rooted in Greek oratory and its influence on 1,700 years of doing church.

But I am also wondering just how much influence has made its way into what we are currently doing via today's strong media pull. My own late evening TV habits as a younger man may reveal what I believe had a significant impact on an historic infatuation with the platform presentation, or center stage.

No matter how long or busy my weekdays, they usually ended as Johnny Carson's sidekick, Ed McMahan, introduced the king of late night television with the famous introduction, "Now, heeere's Johnny!"

Did this type of programming impact at all the way in which I led? Whether it was his culture-current witty monologues, the ageless sketches, or the constant guest interviews, it was and always would be known as the "Johnny Carson Show."

And even if Johnny were absent and left a guest host, which happened more often as the show moved on in years, it was still the consummate entertainer's flagship show. From his comic appearance from behind the curtain, to his golf swing leading to the next segment, it was Johnny's Show.

Who knows what went on behind the scenes—the stage, the set, the staff, the producers, the cameramen, those in charge of lighting, the band, the hundreds of people behind the scenes? But, at the end of the day, the show still belonged to one person, the man at center stage.

A Brief Summary of the Tonight Show[1]

There are many Web sites you can surf to review the detailed history of the famous *Tonight Show* with Johnny Carson, many claiming to be official sites of Johnny Carson. You can even purchase entire sets of DVDs with historic reruns. The basic information and facts here come from the free Web encyclopedia at Wikipedia:

> Carson became host of NBC's *The Tonight Show Starring Johnny Carson,* after Jack Paar quit in October 1962. His announcer and sidekick was Ed McMahon throughout the program. His opening line, "Heeeere's Johnny" became a hallmark.
>
> Most of the later shows began with music and the announcement "Heeeeeere's Johnny!" followed by a brief

monologue by Carson. This was often followed by comedy sketches, interviews, and music. Carson's trademark was a phantom golf swing at the end of his monologues, aimed stage left where the Tonight Show Band was. Guest hosts sometimes parodied that gesture. Bob Newhart rolled an imaginary bowling ball toward the audience.

Paul Anka wrote the theme song ("Johnny's Theme"), a reworking of his "Toot Sweet," given lyrics, renamed "It's Really Love," and recorded by Annette Funicello in 1959. Anka gave Carson co-authorship and they split the royalties for three decades.

The show was originally produced in New York City, with occasional stints in California. It was not live in its early years, although during the 1970s NBC fed the live taping from Burbank to New York via satellite for editing (see below). The program had been done "live on tape" (uninterrupted unless a problem occurred) since the Jack Paar days. In May 1972 the show moved from New York to Burbank, California. Carson often joked about "beautiful downtown Burbank"[6] and referred to "beautiful downtown Bakersfield," which prompted Mayor Mary K. Shell to chide Carson and invite him to her city to see improvements made during the early 1980s.

After the move, Carson stopped doing shows five days a week. Instead, on Monday nights there was a guest host, leaving Carson to do the other four each week. Shows were taped in Burbank at 5:30 p.m. (8:30 p.m. Eastern time) to be shown that evening at 11:30 p.m. Eastern time.

On September 8, 1980, at Carson's request, the show cut its 90-minute format to 60 minutes; Tom Snyder's *Tomorrow* added a half hour to fill the vacant time.

Joan Rivers became the "permanent" guest host from September 1983 until 1986, when she was fired for accepting a competing show on Fox without consulting Carson. *The Tonight Show* returned to using guest hosts, including comic George Carlin. Jay Leno then became the exclusive guest host in fall 1987. Leno stated that although other guest hosts upped their fees, he kept his low, assuring himself the show. Eventually, Monday night was for Leno, Tuesday for the Best of Carson, rebroadcasts usually of a year earlier but occasionally from the 1970s.

Carson retired from show business on May 22, 1992, when he stepped down as host of *The Tonight Show*. His farewell was a major media event, and stretched over several nights. It was often emotional for Carson, his colleagues, and the audiences, particularly the farewell statement he delivered on his 4,531st and final *Tonight Show*.

NBC gave the role of host to the show's then-current permanent guest host, Jay Leno. Leno and David Letterman were soon competing on separate networks."

Even in my early days of searching for significance as a pastor of a local church, the Sunday meeting I presided over often felt like a weekly production, with so much investment of energy, time, and preparation, with "yours truly" as the star. I remember voicing my concerns one day to a friend, who came back a few days later with the remark, "Gary, you know you're right, sometimes it does feel like the Gary Show." We laughed and moved on to the next subject, while that thought about the Sunday flagship show (or meeting) never left.

Over the years I would try to experiment with all kinds of innovative ways to adjust the church meetings to make them more creative, user-friendly, even more participative. But in all my trying those innovative things, like interviewing people in the middle of a meeting, breaking people up into small groups for better discussion, even allowing an occasional guest speaker (or guest host), it was still my church, my meeting, "my show."

And even though short in physical stature, I broke some unwritten law when I stepped off the stage or platform in the church building with the desire to get closer to those I led. Even then, those many years ago, I knew that if I was called to lead, at least my proximity to those I was to lead needed a major overhaul.

Stage Diving for Boomers

But it wasn't easy (nor did it get easier) for me to get off my stage of performing. I had led from there for too many years, and had probably led too well.

I was raised in a home full of preachers. Not just church leaders, or people who could teach, administrate, and lead worship, but good ole' fashioned preachers. Our family gatherings became so known for their sermonizing and verbosity we decided they should be called conferences rather than reunions.

Preaching was the accepted norm and accepted anointing of my day. In the early days of the Pentecostal/evangelical wars, the battle often was over the value of the researched taught word, as opposed to the power of Spirit-anointed preached word.

I even remember how concerned my mother was about my possibly attending a denominational Bible college, as she was convinced it would water down my passion and lessen my anointing when I preached.

Raised in that system, what do you think I aspired to be? Obviously, a good preacher! So off we went, worn Bibles in hand, microphones with very long cords (for mobility and effect in a prewireless generation). If you preached your voice raw or horse, (what we called the "Pentecostal croup"), you could get stronger "amens" in the meetings. And if you could actually lose your voice and develop a consistent raspy tone when you preached all of the time, it was considered a true badge of courage.

When Mom Came to Church

I will never forget when my mother attended a meeting at the first church I led in the early 1970s. She and Dad were only able to be with us for a midweek service. I should have braced myself.

It was one of those smaller meetings, as most midweek gatherings were. That particular night, we had people sitting around tables in our little sanctuary as I led a table-discussion format from a stool without a microphone. Mom? Well, she picked up immediately that I was not boosting my voice through the use of the microphone, I was not using the pulpit, and I was not preaching.

Well, her heart was broken, and it showed. She had trained me to preach. Our dysfunctional style of communication, or lack thereof, was carried on at our little apartment for the next few days after that meeting. It was like trying to ignore the proverbial "elephant in the room," as we cordially visited together with our toned-down, courteous, controlled interactions, or lack thereof, until our cordial goodbyes.

Years on, Mom and I did get some of this communication confusion straightened out as we all learned together that volume and violence were not the best criteria for gauging effective preaching, teaching, or proclamation of any kind, and that the goal is for people to learn, and not just be controlled by overpowering sound. As a family, we even began to admit that some of the old trappings or styles actually hindered the process of learning and for sure lessened retention.

And something else happened during those early years in my first pastorate that God used to set me up for the future. A young man came to me one day to make me an offer. He was new to our church, rather shy but very amiable and kind. He told me that God had spoken to him that he was to be my disciple, my shadow, and my friend. This was not the first time I had heard that, but past experience had taught me that it usually was intertwined with some ulterior motive.

This one sounded and felt different. I knew he really wanted to be my friend. So, for the next few years that was what we tried to develop. We spent good chunks of time together, most of them relaxed, all of them interactive. We debated, ate, laughed, read, shared, prayed, argued together, but did so in such a way that always conveyed honor and understanding. And we became friends.

Years would pass and we moved away from each other, still trying to stay connected, sometimes successful, sometimes not. I realize now, that even back then, God was offering me a new model of being with those I lead, a "chaordic" model, where mutual-mentoring would help us both to grow.

As a young pastor I had been warned by my father to not get close to people in the church, as they would discover your faults, and to stay clear of any proposed friendships from other clergy in your city because they were competition. So, to actually pursue a friendship with someone from the flock was a big step.

It was also during those early days that my own ego evolution was taking place. All of the pastors I associated with had what I called a one-stringed guitar. When we got together for ministers' meetings or local conferences; it was always about one thing, church growth. It was all we spoke of, ate, read about, and lived for. We spent hours having "shop talk" around the tools of our trade to make us better pastors, all geared toward gathering more people and building bigger facilities.

First, it was the sound equipment or printing devices that we invested in. As the years passed, it would require more sound support, more equipment, and eventually entire systems that included monitors, theater lighting, large screens, cameras, typing, editing, PowerPoint projectors, and even direct feeds for the satellite screens to the overflow rooms. All along, this was evolving into more meetings, larger campuses, and even multisite expansions.

And, of course, to pull this all off meant the expansion of the production staff or support team. So the machine grew—teachers, greeters, parking lot attendants, coffee baristas, bookstore helpers, children's ministry workers, ministry teams, and the rest of the media ministry drones just to make the Sunday meeting happen. It included pep talks in between (what we called "staff meetings"), mainly meant to motivate each new batch of "roadies," because the show must go on.

Someone calculated that 80 percent of all time, staff energy, and finances in a local church are required to produce and sustain the Sunday (or weekend) flagship meeting. I even know of churches with multiple-meeting weekends that use at least one of the week-end meetings as a dress rehearsal for the production team so they can time and edit the meetings to best fit into the remaining time slots—all of this time, energy, and resources to set up, stage, and venue a form and a style of communication that at its best seems to produce so few lasting results.

The Sermonator or Facilitator?

So, here you are the lead pastor, or the senior communicator, or the "sermonator" if you will, living behind your pulpit, your sacred desk, that itself is an ancient relic or prop from early Greek theater that the ancient sophists used to pound to emphasize the points of their oratory debate. You have all of the required accoutrements required to enhance that elusive 45-minute presentation, to deliver that main meal in the sanctuary to inspire the saints.

But what do we really know about the power of the spoken word? Speech is a challenging animal, in that it is both linear and unpaceable. In preaching, you can't skip around too much and remain very cohesive, and if you speed up too fast "to cut to the chase," you often need translation.

And why do we preachers "come to conclusion" so many times in the same sermon? Could it be that we really don't know where to stop, because many times we weren't even sure where we began? What do we do with the fact that when the speaker covers a subject people don't know, listeners get bored? And when the speaker covers something people have never heard, they get lost?

Statistics have been floating around for years that within 20 minutes of hearing a message, people forget 40 percent of the content; they lose 60 percent within half a day of the message; and within one week the average listener can recall only 10 percent of what was said. And even that retention is because of the addition of large screens and fill-in-the-blank inserts in the bulletin.

So, if in general, preaching works so poorly, why do we keep putting it forth as an ideal form of disciple making? I know my own preaching days are not over, as I continue to travel to the nations. In many of the venues I go to they only know how to invite me to a lead conference or a seminar or a workshop, which they often help facilitate through multimedia support.

It is just that for years I have asked myself, "Am I making disciples?" I really want to make disciples and not just gather listeners.

So that means I must address my own frustrations and wrestle with my own convictions. And even as I write, I am currently trying to use my schedule, and my opportunities, especially within leadership development, to spend more and more time in casual conversation, with more and more intentional face time, with more and more smaller groups where we are discovering God's truths together over meals and open discussions, rather than waiting for the next big crusade.

Endnote

1. http://en.wikipedia.org/wiki/Johnny_Carson.

CHAPTER 2

TURNING DOWN CELEBRITY STATUS

NO ONE STARTS OUT SEEKING to obey God's call to servanthood full of grandiose and glamorous ideas of ego-driven success, starving for the spotlight at center stage. The call of God itself is too holy, too lofty, too daunting, too heart wrenching, even too fearful.

We are looking for a place to serve and even a place to sacrifice, following the leading of our Lord and Master, who didn't even have a place to lay His head.

But like Israel, once they settled into the land, success takes us places we don't expect, and the next thing we know, those humble beginnings can give way to the private tailors, personal assistants, assigned parking, tagged and preferred seating, body guards, limos and green rooms.

No More High Chairs for High Leaders

I'll never forget my early days of traveling in Asia where I was seated on a throne-styled carved chair that had silk slippers placed on matching silk pillows in front of the chair. Years later, I would visit that same church. The platform or stage was empty except for the worship team, while the pastor roamed among the worshiping saints.

And at least for my taste, that cultural shift better represented what I believe the Gospel or good news of Jesus is and how it relates to real people.

Not everyone agrees with my assessment that there remains too much pomp and circumstance in today's church. Many feel these trappings are necessary to correctly represent a big and powerful God. Some, especially Westerners, would suggest that it's even necessary to attract the people of today's media culture by using all of the trappings they are accustomed to. Because we are all conditioned, or trained by the cinema, or the theatre, and the professional shows and bands, that our consumers expect, even demand these first-class productions.

As a result, local churches compete to produce the best show in town. The only problem is that the people we are trying to attract seem no longer impressed with the show. Not only can they find better entertainment elsewhere, there appears to be a standard reality that a huge exodus of people are now exiting the weekend church as we know it, in order to find something else, something simpler and even more authentic.

This presents a great opportunity for us to find new wineskins for the wine! We have good reason to step away from our center stages and begin our walk among the sheep of His pasture (see Psalm 100).

Human leadership must become less visible and more of a sacred influence. We need fewer inspired speakers and more inspired listeners, fewer teachers and more fathers. Church is not even about the meetings anymore. It is about that relational context and the proximity of one generation of leaders realigning to the next generation.

While leadership is a strategic placement of God, it must come from a new place, a new place to lead, a new place to live, a new place to learn, a new place to follow.

This is not another poor attempt at redefining leadership; instead, this is an invitation for leaders to come from behind a series of barricades that hide them and even keep them at a safe but artificial distance and learn to walk alongside those they lead in a partnership and through a discovery process that both changes the leader as well as the one being led. It is a process of learning to lead by learning to walk with, laugh with, stroll with, and even follow.

Redefining or Repositioning?

It is more of a repositioning, rather than a redefining of leadership. But in the repositioning there is a stark redefinition. To be sure, the styles, the focus, the intentions are very different between relational, chaordic community and distanced, institutional leading.

- One takes time, the other takes a text.

- One is about relating, the other about research.

- One requires living in context of a series of life moments, the other requires the delivery of a good sermon series.

- One leans on the disciplined commitment to the formation of a life, the other justifies the continual dispensing of the most current information on the subject.

- One requires that we become inspiring listeners, the other requires we are inspired speakers.

- One leads by walking with or coming alongside others, the other leads alone, in the spotlight, center stage, yet in institutional isolation.

Like Escorts at Weddings

Learning to lead chaordically is like learning to be an escort at a wedding.

At the wedding, the escort does not sit in the back of the room pointing and shouting to the guests where they need to sit. Nor does he leave the wedding site, abdicating his responsibility by letting everyone simply sit where they choose.

At the wedding, the escort knows distinctly where each guest belongs. With his help, each guest succeeds to either the bride or groom's side, even avoiding the chairs that are reserved for family and special guests. As the escort draws near the guest, he extends his arm, his help, and his aid, and escorts the guest toward their seat, guaranteeing that each and every guest finds their precise destination.

And all of this is done for the purpose of honoring the bride and the bridegroom; John said,

He who has the bride is the bridegroom; but the friend of the bridegroom, who stands and hears him, rejoices greatly because of the bridegroom's voice. Therefore the joy of mine is fulfilled. He must increase, but I must decrease (John 3:29-30).

And as Peter later punctuates,

Shepherd the flock of God which is among *you, serving as overseers, not by constraint but willingly, not for dishonest gain but eagerly; nor as being lords* over *those entrusted to you, but being* examples *to the flock; and when the Chief Shepherd appears you will receive the crown of glory that does not fade away* (1 Peter 5:2-4, Emphasis mine).

Throughout the remainder of this book, you are invited to lead among, not from and not over, those entrusted to you. You are invited into a way of leading that honors the Bride and the Bridegroom and, of course, follows the lead of the Chief Shepherd.

Leaders, shepherds, overseers, or whatever you are called, welcome to "Usher University" to learn the protocol of the wedding. Whether pastor or parents, businessmen or bosses, learning to treat those you influence and employ and lead by "coming alongside" like an usher at a wedding, makes the Bride healthy and the Bridegroom happy.

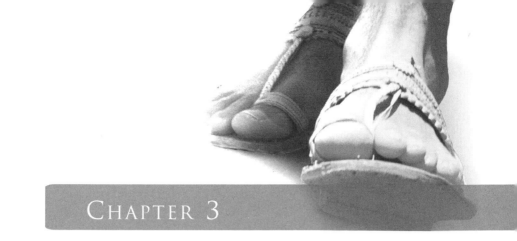

CHAPTER 3

WHERE DID JESUS LEAD?

WHO WAS THAT walking, strolling, wandering Master Teacher? Who was that peripatetic Rabbi whose walks turned into life lessons and whose strolls turned into blasts of transformational truths? Who was that storyteller, so skilled at communicating, that it was though His stage props miraculously appeared at the maximum moment just to make His point? Who was that masked man, anyway?

For the woman at the well in John 4, Jesus operated with a word of knowledge and prophecy; Matthew 16 becomes a serious Q & A moment as He used an arousing survey that released the truth about His identity. To the blind man at Jericho it was mud and spittle; to a demoniac in Mark's gospel it was an exorcism into a herd of pigs that provided a regional evangelism assignment.

To the street walker, His pausing in a home for a meal meant an appointed anointing with costly perfume, to a man blind from birth in John 9, it meant an apologetics of generational questions gone bad, and on a stormy sea, it was an afternoon nap and a weather rebuke that produced both faith and fear in His disciples.

In Mark 6, it was the gathering of a large hungry crowd, and a small boy's lunch of sardines and muffins turned into a bread and fish buffet miracle that caused the crowd to want to make Him king.

To a tree out of season it was a lesson on faith and fruit bearing, and to a precocious child set in their midst it meant a revelation of the character of childlikeness.

And where did all of these learning moments happen? In a classroom? In a school hall? In the assembly hall of the local synagogue? And were these a preset series of preplanned systematic theology points that needed to be completed through the fill-in-the-blanks bulletin inserts or notebooks?

What did it mean for Jesus to walk among His friends, doing the Father's will and being constantly available and ready to debrief with questions, probing ideas, interaction and the constant presence of miracles, signs, wonders, and healing? What about all of these parables, and what about all the stories?

I remember a friend saying to me once, "Gary, do you really want to do WWJD? Pick a dozen guys, live with them day in and day out, pouring your life into them, and see what that experiment produces."

Jesus the "Sheep-Man"

The cultural context of the agrarian metaphors from Jesus' style of leading are still meant to impact and instruct us. They are there to nudge us to embrace an ancient Middle Eastern model of Jesus, the Good Shepherd, the Great Shepherd sheep walker. His kingdom analogies and His conspicuous lifestyle were meant to provide more than just a pattern, or a set grid. They were to offer us a leadership modality that would be ours for generations to come.

All of this begins at His birth announcement: *"Behold, a virgin shall be with child, and bear a Son, and they shall call His name Immanuel," which is translated, "God with us"* (Matt. 1:23). *"And the Word became flesh and dwelt among us, and we beheld His glory, the glory as of the only begotten of the Father, full of grace and truth"* (John 1:14).

God with us, God among us, God near us, God touchable to us. A tactile God, a God with texture, a God with flesh on. This is the context for His beginning, the context for His earthly ministry, and if we would dare to follow Him, the context for how we are to be to others. This incarnational model is what sets the ministry of Jesus apart from hierarchy, distance, control, manipulation, and coercion.

Somehow, the very essence of biblical shepherding seems to get twisted with us through this whole idea of moving the sheep. Although it is about care, for us it becomes about the challenge of the move. Although it is about the handling of individual sheep, for us it always turns into massive drive of "herds" or "flocks" of sheep. We often confuse the Middle Eastern model (the flock of 99) with the Western or occidental view of a commercial shepherd who gets his sheep to market. Like *City Slickers*, we want them to go, usually by our driving them, using either the crafty assistance of our well-trained dogs, or our modern riders on the all-terrain vehicles.

I was raised in an agricultural community. The edges of the desert town I lived in as a child were covered with alfalfa fields as flocks of sheep were moved through our region for both pasture and clearing. As a young lad I seldom recall ever seeing that lone ancient shepherd with faithful and sturdy staff just meandering among the flock. I do remember the temporary fences, lots of small trailers or campers, the sounds of the specialized sheep dogs, and the small four-wheel loaders. This was the trade of professional sheepherders and the sounds of their modern equipment.

Jesus provides us with an image of the oriental shepherd; more appropriately called a "sheep man." He walks among His flock, with that classic picture of the prodigal lamb over his shoulders, at night sleeping with his flock and during the day interacting with the other shepherds who cared for their sheep, as well as patiently leading them to good and safe pasture.

Shepherds Are Not Cowboys

True shepherds are not like cowboys who think they know where the sheep ought to be, and so by force, trail drives them to their destination. This kind of cowboy leader tends to (1) be rigid and dominate; (2) create ego paths as he goes; (3) require and demand a highly supportive bureaucracy from the ranch hands to pull off the drive and to adequately gauge the speed of the flock; (4) and, often, because of striving for a certain measurable pace to be functionally and operationally successful, be driven to compete as he races against other flocks.

Cowboys are drivers, leading for positional and political gain, running roughshod over flocks that don't follow and don't produce, rather than laying their lives down for the sheep.

Shepherds Are Not Hirelings

True shepherds are not like hirelings who overreact to the fear of self-preservation, becoming easily distracted by the sounds and smells of the flock's enemies, the flock's predators. Where cowboys are driven by their own narcissism to lead, hirelings tend to be controlled by their own fears. Too easily startled, too easily scattered, and way too quick to change directions in midstream due to their own agendas, hirelings seem to lead when it is convenient for them, when they are emotionally ready, when the pay is right, or when the sheep serve their personal purpose.

Hirelings are cowards, prostituting their call by jeopardizing the safety of the flock for the emotion of the moment, rather than laying down their lives for the sheep.

A true shepherd's robes smell of his sheep, his shoes are coated with their droppings. His lifestyle is measured by his long hours of serving and caring. He walks among them so they feel safe, he lies next to them at night so they can sleep well, he even makes sounds in the night, which douses their fears and covers the sounds of their hunters. He touches them often, petting them, pouring oil into their wounds, and embracing them. He consistently counts them, not to boast in a head count, but to make sure they are all safe. All along their journey they are learning his voice, his tones, his ways, and learning to lean into him as their trust is built as he serves them.

Jesus said, *"Feed my sheep."* The Great Shepherd's Psalm 23 is still the most read of all Old Testament passages. And He still leads you and me by *"still waters,"* and He still *"restores my soul."*

But listen; at the end of the day, sheep usually don't make good trophies. You won't find a floppy lamb's head mounted in a hunter's lodge next to the exotic boar's head, or the massive swordfish fought over for hours off the back of the specially rigged prize fishing vessel. The obvious nature of sheep, that some have even called "being geographically impaired," or "geographical morons," is that of a tender species of animal that requires a unique and conspicuous style of care.

Called sheep 43 times in the Bible, we are all cut out of that sheep cloth that needs to be led rather than driven, coached rather than commandeered, and cared for instead of controlled or commanded.

Because the natural and universal inclination of man is the tendency to give priority to self-interests ahead of the needs of others, we have to face the spirit of this age as self-centered and egocentric. To describe the general attitude that prevails in today's culture regarding self, we could say it is *centric.* Centric is man at the center of man's focus and it fosters immature and selfish thinking. And it is too often the reason why we pursue performance-driven leadership built on status and outcomes rather than resting in God's authority and anointing to release others through our ministries through a dream-sensitive style of leading.

Mature thinking is more *radic.* Not in the classic meaning of radical, but "radic" in that it radiates out, rather than centering in. Christ was a "radic" thinker and liver, serving God's purposes and plans, even now at God's right hand continuing to serve us through His intercession. He was not a cowboy, dominating, driving, concerned only with the operational dynamics of his herd. And He was never a hireling, swayed by His emotions, but always a lover who laid it all down for His sheep.

He was a "sheep man." Jesus was not just investing in the merchandizing potential of His "sheared" little flock. Instead, it was each sheep's potential that interested Him. As they followed Him, they were kept safe and secure. In this way we, following His lead, learn to lead among and to lead differently.

Following Jesus' Lead

To get down to this Jesus who "walked in the flesh," means to hear the objections of His culture as He stepped on the scene at the end of His third decade. Where angelic choirs might have sung His aria, His introduction, the rest of His story was not a popularity contest and leans hard toward obscurity, rejection, and betrayal.

Even when He announced Himself at Nazareth, it was a total disconnect. When His synagogue sermon shouted that *today this Scripture has been fulfilled in your hearing"* (Luke 4:21) they had already passed judgment and could not see beyond the familial suspicion of this boy from a local town, the son of a carpenter.

Even though they had spent hundreds of years preoccupied and looking for the Messiah, any of those who were listening to be impressed totally missed Him. To them He was the illegitimate son of Joseph, (see Luke 4:22). In their pharisaical minds, He lacked the resume, and the necessary credentials of someone with royal lineage. In their minds, He had to live with all of Isaiah's prophecy. Not just the one in Isaiah 61, but also in chapter 53, where it precariously delineated, *"He has no stately form or majesty that we should look upon Him, nor appearance that we should be attracted to Him"* (Isa. 53:2).

All of this is seems a far cry from the pursuit of senior leaders today, whose public personas are judged by how they carry themselves, along with their image ratings as the congregation and the TV audience grows. While called to be servants and shepherds, our high mortality rate comes all to quickly from the outside media pressures of today's performances.

If we are to follow Jesus' lead, it begins with the humble presentation of one overlooked, rejected, underestimated, yet even more humbled by the sheer honor of the call to be a "sheep man" among the flock of God.

Sheep to Sheep

There are, of course, some built-in limitations as we take the sheep/shepherd metaphor to its end. In the sheep/shepherd metaphor, there exists the natural tension of the two species. In the parables and the stories, it is Jesus the Sheep Man with us, the sheep. But we are all the sheep of His pasture, whether considered leaders or followers (see Psalm 100). And if we dare to lead, we must inevitably follow as well, always "sheep with sheep."

So this idea of coming alongside someone to lead becomes even more evident and clear. We lead from their level, their plane, their height, and their posture, eating at their pasture, all being led by Him. Shoulder to shoulder, face to face, we lead others as we move alongside one another, as we lean on, as we influence, and as we see each other at a common perspective, at a common level.

All along adjusting our direction and our communication from one sheep to another, ultimately being led by Him and to Him, the Good Shepherd, the Great Shepherd, the Sheep Man. This Sheep

Man, that lays down His life for His sheep, bedding down and securing those 99, only to make His way at that late hour to find just that one that is lost.

During His life Jesus reserved some of His harshest speech for religious leaders who maintained their very obvious distinction-driven lifestyle that too often kept them away from the masses, sometimes far away. On more than one occasion it broke his heart—a shepherd, seeing His people shepherdless (see Mark 6:34).

So raw was this division between leaders and followers that the Pharisees even used something called *Corban,* an irresponsible financial copout insulating and isolating them for caring of their parents (see Mark 7:9-13). The whole idea of living as a Pharisee is that of a separatist, thriving in religious exclusivity. And Jesus, incarnating the exact opposite of this spirit of separation (Immanuel: *"God with us"* (Matt. 1:23)) constantly confronts those religious bigots with His searing remarks toward their arrogance.

On top of that, Jesus abhorred the name game that so often propped up their insolence. He lambasts them for their preoccupation with what others called them (see Matthew 23), and at times conspicuously downplayed His own worthy title until it was time for His prophetic revelation to become more known.

In His own survey in Matthew 16, after Peter spoke by revelation that *"Jesus was the Christ, the Son of the Living God,"* even after that, He nowhere required that they address Him from His truly revealed title.

Always in the company of those who frustrated His critics, Jesus' own reputation was stained with the ongoing accusation of His being "with," being too often among those He led, *"The Son of man came eating and drinking, and they say, 'Look, a glutton and a winebibber, a friend of tax collectors and sinners!"* (Matt. 11:20).

Jesus modeled chaordic leading "among" from the very beginning, not leading from some lofty space, or place. He who was equal with God becomes flesh, steps down from that heavenly throne room and becomes the self-emptying one (see Philippians 2) the one with not even a pillow for rest. In His *kenosis* (His self-emptying) as seen in the litany in Philippians 2, in His serving, in His walking away from all that was His in the heavenly realm, He models the attitude we are called to emulate. He abandons Heaven to show us Heaven on earth and how to lead among, reserving some of His harshest words for anyone who might *"lord over"* His flock like the Gentiles (see Mark 10:42).

In addressing the leadership ceiling that feeds a broken culture and trickles into a broken church, we must all confront a systemic structure that tolerates isolated leadership and abandoned followers. These trends must be challenged for both the protection of the sheep and even the safety of the leaders and the glory of the Sheep Man.

CHAPTER 4

LEADERSHIP OR FOLLOWERSHIP?

IT HAS BECOME A SIMPLE FORMULA in the physics of life, if you don't "follow," you can't "lead." Any true chaordic leadership will often feel like following. For you to so lead requires a manifest unity alongside another's vision, alongside another's calling and alongside another's gifting. To so serve that one you are walking with will often remind you that it is his or her vision that you are following, which is actually your gift of leadership to them.

My personal kudos, and a standing ovation to anyone willing to risk current institutional forms in your quest for relational ones. I honor you because I know it is a very costly experiment, and not very flattering to one's own recognized leadership giftings and calling.

Staying on the side of institutional leading with all of its perks and visibility seems much easier on the ego than stepping into the shadow of someone else's potential gifting in order to make room for them and their destiny.

It seems far more appealing to be the focal point at center stage than lost in the crowd of mutual mentoring. The very antithesis of leading through today's systems with its massive pulpit appeal and star quality lifestyle is to come alongside some neophyte struggling on their journey.

Wolfgang Simson, in his now-classic *Houses That Change the World*, reminds us:

> In Hebrew culture, the traditional teacher was the father, gathered around the table with his family at the meal. It was in that living context amidst the ordinary things of life, sharing stories and recounting the lessons of the day that the father would speak into the lives of his children.[1]

> Teaching was traditionally geared to show somebody how to do something, and to explain why things are the way they are. The goal of the interaction was not to increase knowledge, but to train people to obey and serve God and His purposes."

So that the goal of this kind of relational teaching is not to deliver the systematic A–Z set of doctrine, but to present a disciple, mature through a spirit of quick obedience and a developed, gift-oriented ministry. And not merely for a ministry inside four walls, or a ministry divorced from daily life in the real world of ships, and sails and sealing wax, cabbages and kings, but precisely a life engaged with real people in their ordinary contexts—a missional and incarnational expression of with-ness. Greek philosophy shares, "thought is not meaningful without action; and action is not meaningful without friendship."

As Jesus said in the Great Commission, we were to teach them to obey everything Jesus commanded us (see Matthew 28:20).

Jesus in the Hood

Eugene Peterson's *The Message* states it well: "*The Word became flesh and blood and moved into the neighborhood.*" This seems to be the operating system for the Jesus model of His earthly journey. With a small cadre, a simple mobile community of faith, what Jesus did was to teach them to do, and He did all of it by moving into the neighborhood.

This Middle Eastern style of leading begins by a decision to enter someone else's context. As they say in Africa, "Will you walk with me?" which does not translate as a tender stroll or short walk, but a life walk.

When I traveled to South Africa, many years ago, most of the villages were full of women, young boys, and old men as the work force had moved to the South or the Cape to work in the mines. One of the elders left in one of these villages was an elderly Xhosa man named Tupana. Tupana was a walking preacher who, though already in his early eighties, continued to walk the terrain of the Transkei, a then-unincorporated part of South Africa.

When he asked me one day, "Will you walk with me?" that was not an invitation for a cool afternoon stroll, it was a challenge to join him in some kind of marathon that could last possibly for days to progress to another village or preaching point.

So, I knew that those words really meant, "Will you enter my life journey with me?" I had been duly forewarned at the tribe's embrace to this white leader when they issued me a hand-made cane and a wide brimmed hat. Both of these items tools of the trade that were meant for taking some long life walks.

There is a great scene in Jim Carrey's movie *Bruce Almighty,* immediately after the hilarious soup-splitting scene in the diner. God shows up and invites Bruce to walk with him awhile. He explains the rules, cracks a joke or two, and affirms Bruce's right to ask questions. Later, when we see the two again in the wide, white expanse of the office tower, we see them mopping the floor in a kind of synchronized dance. Walking together and learning to work together, they fall into the same rhythm. This is what shared life creates.

This idea of hanging out with others over a life-long commitment to someone else's journey seems so archaic to twenty-first century faith. It was in another era that the idea of an ethos of fellow travelers on their journey together was most successful.

The Primitive Church

In the original classic first written in 1901 and newly released in 2008, *The Church: The Divine Ideal,*[2] George Dana Boardman addresses what he calls preconceptions that get us in trouble when thinking about the Church. He states:

> We must remember at the very outset that our King Himself while here on earth never commanded His followers to "organize a church; never even hinted any model of a church as an ecclesiastical institution, and

that He Himself used the word "church" but three times, referring in each case to the "church" as a spiritual company rather than an ecclesiastical organization.

In describing the mission of the Church, Boardman basically calls it a Child of Circumstances. He goes on to demand that it is not the mission of the Church to enjoy herself. She is neither a dormitory; nor a junto; nor a library; nor a museum; nor an obelisk; nor a bureau; nor a treadmill; nor a wailing place, but the mission of the Church is to serve God by serving man.

Imagine redefining Church today, or reinventing Church, or even reincarnating the Church, as Wolfgang Simson describes in his newest book *The House Church Book*.[3] He takes care in his memory of seeing the Church as a "supernatural invention, endowed with God's gift of immortality—a means to disciple each other, and make the life of Jesus rub off on each other."

To return to incarnational Christianity means to return to a simple company of men and women who happen to catch up with each other on their common journey, and surrender together to proverbially "walk the walk." This is a wandering group of pilgrims who live within the constraints and commitments to stick it out with each other through thick and thin, through all of the torrential tests and blessed stages of the journey as a lifelong community of faith.

Not a fearful company, not a shy community, and not a hovering or shaking community. But a spiritually endowed brigade that together face the forces of darkness, deception, and destruction, watching each other's backs at all times and sharing in both the tears and the victories of pilgrimage.

Endnotes

1. Wolfgang Simson, *Houses That Change the World* (Emmelsbull, Germany: OM, 1999), 83, 84.

2. George Dana Boardman, *The Church: The Divine Ideal* (Shippensburg, PA: Destiny Image Publishers, 2008), 19, 61.

3. Wolfgang Simson, *The House Church Book* (Carol Stream, IL: Barna Books, 2009), Preface.

CHAPTER 5

PRACTICES OR PRINCIPLES?

IT COULD BE THAT some of this confusion about how and where to best lead is related to our classic, historic approach to the Scriptures. In the modern system of academia Western Church leaders have all been honed to be working wordsmiths and have learned to approach the Bible as an answer book, a kind of spiritual Motor's Manual, rather than a lens that points us to the greater Reality of God and an invitation to enter the dialogue.

We have largely lost the sense of the Greek word for truth, *alethiea*, which is not a list of scientific propositions that are testable in some laboratory experiment, but a relational category that has to do with trust and faith. We can trust that what God says is true, and that His words lead us into a covenant relationship of mystery and discovery. But in our empirical mind-set, our systems of truth are stuck in our heads, along with our logic, our rationale, and our sciences. Especially as we are ingrained in our academic hermeneutical approach to systematic theology.

To a fault, our modern approach to exegesis even has been buttressed by our Sunday one-hour meeting mentality, a context that only allows time for the precise delivery of a litany of steps or principles. Have we yet learned that a one- or two-hour meeting that does not allow for honest discussion, stimulating debate, or multi-imputed conclusions, holds few signs of true discipleship and empowerment?

As Jim Henderson notes in his great little book, *Jim and Casper Go To Church*,

> Jesus didn't just teach principles, He taught practices. He gave people something to do. He didn't just teach them about forgiveness, He told them to forgive their debtors. He didn't just talk about love as a concept (eros, phileo, storge and agape); He told them to love their enemies. He didn't just tell people to think about changing their behaviors, He told them to repent (change their actions). Sure it's challenging, but it doesn't take a weekend seminar to understand what He means.

> As the teaching profession has risen to its place of primacy in the evangelical church, so also has the focus on principles: because that is how teachers think and that is how teachers present. With the proliferation of "The Principles of Everything You Would Ever Want to Know About Anything" seminars, and the thousands of "How-To" books, and the thriving cult of leadership and leadership manuals, it has become painfully obvious that what we need is not more information, but more formation. We need to learn once again to minor in principles and major in practices.

When learning something new (like riding a bike or parallel parking,) the required movements feel awkward and counterintuitive. Under normal circumstances, we might even do the opposite of what we are told to do. We have to practice the movements in order to make them part of our everyday lives, and we typically have someone running alongside of us for a while until we find our bearings. This isn't unlike the routine of a pianist learning the scales. For a while it's daily repetition: ordinary and humdrum. Then one day the scales are left behind because the music is in the fingers.[1]

I am an evangelist at heart, and I do believe in the Great Commission, but I also desire deeply to live in a community of faith that embodies and incarnates that message. I just wonder how much of the power of that message of the Good News comes through the latest evangelism trends, or comes out of being rightly related to my Heavenly Father and to His people, the Body of Christ?

As one who has attempted to do everything possible to create this kind of necessary unity that would emulate Psalm 133 and fulfill Christ's High-priestly prayer in John 17, I am still wondering how much greater impact we could make in our culture, if we got caught truly in love with God and each other?

A good reread of Jesus' prayer, *"that they all may be one, as You Father are in me"* (John 17:21), is one that pushes in front of me the possibility of a relationship of intimacy and oneness that may be more about the vertical one between He and Father, rather than an exclusive inference to the horizontal one between you and me.

I simply am thinking out loud as to whether we may have over-stated the horizontal unity and missed the vertical intimacy. I do know this, that when the vertical relationship of intimacy with my Father is working, that automatically sheds light and dynamic on my horizontal ones with others.

I also think that when our relationship of intimacy is broken with the Father, it puts a strain on my fellowship life and creates a very difficult environment for any true or meaningful fellowship with one another. I have come to call this the "sucking sound of fellowship." Get some Christians together who do not have an active personal history with God, and their need for community is so out of whack, out of balance, or out of proportion, that it will "scream for too much community" until that need for intimacy with God is restored.

The current migration of believers from fellowship to fellowship is very likely a search for Him rather than each other. And as we pursue Him, our love, our patience, and our way of being with each other radically changes.

Moving those we lead into an actual discipleship or an apprentice mode of "doing" what Jesus said comes through an agreement to walk together for that long haul (see Amos 3:3). It initially means spending lots of time together along the way. Its early demands mean lots of talks and lots of walks, lots of listening, lots of coffee, lots of time of just hanging out and being together, and lots of leaning on each other until the time when we can safely see the other person has learned to lean on Jesus.

In fact, when that interpersonal transference or counter-transference happens in our relationships, it can be a sign that our relationship has become more about codependency on each other rather than interdependence on the Father, and how He is showing up in each of our lives. It always has to be about Him, leading people to Him, directing people to Him, and what He is doing in us and through us.

Two Traps

There remain two precarious traps for Christians and discipleship. We do believe that God's Word is our unchanging standard for life and practice, and yet it is still possible to fall into the wary snares of either "knowing without doing" or "doing without knowing."

One is based on our habit of trafficking in "unlived truths," where we preach a good sermon, make a good point, research the subject as to appear as an expert, but really don't know by personal habit what we are talking about. We really don't know because there is no true "knowing without doing." We simply don't do or haven't done what we say, so we really lack experience in living out the truth and end up have nothing to say.

There is a big difference between creating a teaching series on divine healing and healing the sick—a big difference between making a good talk of devotions and being a person of devotion.

The other trap is this habitual exercise of outward obedience, with a high drive for conformity in community, doesn't bear fruit because it is born out of little internal processing or revelation. That is dangerous when Scripture and truth are necessary to really ignite our actions.

External adherence, or doing with no heart, is very easily the product of today's monitored peer-pressure accountability.

Whether it is generosity, worship, fasting, prayer, or the study of God's Word, it just doesn't cut it, if it's all outward performance with no deep heart conviction and revelation.

What might even be more abominable than God's creatures not worshiping Him is a lot of outward religious expressions of worship with a dead heart. That seemed to bother the Father greatly in Jesus' teaching on worship in John 4.

All of the things God has called us to do can be done selfishly, for the wrong motives, yet they are still done for the approval of men, done to be accepted, done out of fear or manipulation—all of the time lacking God's heart as needed to be revealed behind these activities.

Jesus, of course, reserved some of His harshest words for those whose activities were done again and again, mainly to be seen of men, yet in the end it was merely the exterior lacquer, or the outer veneer or façade with death inside.

In much the same way, have we placed the Great Commission over the First Commandment? Are we guilty of either the "knowing without doing" or the "doing without knowing?" And are we being called back to a new kind of relationship, a new kind of relating, and a new way of being with God first and then with each other, rather than just being jazzed about the newest, hottest evangelistic method or tool?

We have such a great need for fathers who, because of their own experiential history, know not only what to do, but how to live. We need journeymen, who have well-used compasses and who not only know the direction, but have the longevity and the mileage to back it up. They know what to do and they know why they do it. They know the One they do it for.

> *I write to you, fathers, because you have* known *Him who is from the beginning* (1 John 2:13, Emphasis added).

> ... *That I may* know *Him and the power of His resurrection, and the fellowship of His sufferings, being conformed to His death* (Philippians 3:10, Emphasis added).

As leaders, if we don't learn early the snare of these traps, we are doomed to repeat them in our disciples.

Endnote

1. Jim Henderson and Matt Casper, *Jim and Casper Go To Church* (Carol Stream, IL. Tyndale, 2007), Introduction, xxxiii, xxxiv.

CHAPTER 6

LEADING BY LISTENING

ON OCCASIONS I DO SPEAK to larger groups, preach a sermon series, share a teaching, or whatever nomenclature fits your glossary of terms. Sometime when this happens I will make eye contact with someone in the crowd who seems especially engaged and I think to myself, "Gee, I wonder what it would be like if I was sitting across from this individual over a cup of coffee, and sharing these same thoughts that are coming out in my lecture?" And I wonder how that would change the dynamics and the delivery of this truth transaction if it became the interactive experience of a couple of people on the same page?

I know the difference would be incredible. Imagine those mutual moments of truth as you experience their part of the equation. In our delivery styles, have we settled for the message exchange and not the mutual experience? That is what chaordic leadership is about—creating a different kind of atmosphere through which to learn. The learning is mutual because the exchange is built on relationships, so the entire experience is about each other's contribution. When that happens, everything changes. To enter into this new relationship, it requires that we learn to speak a new language, and that we learn to lead by listening.

I know that some of this shift could possibly happen even in our larger meetings. We need not forfeit the pursuit of intimacy just because of the size of the crowd. Dialogue versus monologue is often an attitude and not an issue of logistics. We can create an amazing atmosphere of interactive participation by how we approach truth and how we ask questions, even while appearing to be making statements.

The Jacobsens (Wayne and Clay) in *Authentic Relationships* tell the story of going to a men's breakfast where the participants pulled out scorecards on how many days during the previous week they had read Scripture, witnessed to an unbeliever, or "hit their knees" before "hitting the shower." They were holding each other accountable to disciplines they thought important. And note that as sincere as they may have been to encourage one another, they were sincerely wrong[1].

I confess that most of my own discipleship history, particularly in the early days of being a pastor came more out of a strained accountability, watchdog-type relationship. I do take seriously the assignment to walk out a daily lifestyle of fruitful disciplines that cause me to water and work well on my personal "inner garden," including spending time with God through solitude, silence, prayer, and meditating on Scripture.

And while I desire to share my personal delights and history with God when I am mentoring or walking with someone, ultimately these are not just teaching or discipleship tools. They are how I relate to God; they are about my relationship with my Father. I like to model these things so they, too, might eventually know and walk in them. I can tell others about them, and even show them how I do them, but I want to do that in such an atmosphere of curiosity and mutuality that eventually those I lead are pressed to practice them on their own, willing to develop their own personal history with God. Years ago, I wrote this in one of my journal entries, "Your destiny is hidden in your daily routines."

The Emmaus Experience

Like those brothers on the Emmaus Road, at some point their encounter with Jesus created a mutual context, a mutual experience. Their hearts "burned" within them because there was a moment when both information and revelation collided. So whether you are one on one or in a larger equipping setting, you are looking for that synergism of "heart and head" and not just the personal satisfaction that comes from a well-hit ball or a well-delivered homily.

We enter into these pregnant moments of truth with others knowing that the principles of seedtime and harvest will kick in. People seem to tire of our encounters with them as we do one more discipleship lesson, one more fill-in-the-blanks moment, and they begin to hunger for a moment, or look for an epiphany when something we are discussing, something we are chewing over, comes really alive. The light goes on, and that truth is forever lodged where we "know" it, and not just "hear" it.

To habitually do for others what God has called them to do is the highest form of theft and idolatry. This idea that people leave churches or ministries because they are "not being fed" appalls me. What a sick picture of a mother bird eating and passing on her regurgitated food to her young. It is not the goal of leadership to "feed" others. Shepherds lead sheep to pasture to find good food to eat, but the sheep themselves must ultimately consume the food for themselves or there is no nourishment. The goal of all biblical training is not serving up a meal as much as it is creating a hunger, which manifests itself in well-trained "self-feeders."

That is another reason why this addiction to someone else's sermons, or eating patterns, or even meal preparation must stop. I can't eat for you, study for you, and worship for you, or even pray for you when God has called you to do so many of these things for yourself. But I can tell you where to go to grab a healthy sandwich, and sometimes time well spent can help you grab and get and learn some of the same basic disciplines and delights that complement a lifestyle in God. And if you learn these things from me, it is my hope that they will eventually enlarge you and grow you, and, yes, delight you as He leads you.

My own version of *lectio divina* (Latin for "divine reading," or "holy reading"), or what I call "reading until He speaks," has been one of the greatest joys of my own journey.

I look forward to those times when I get alone, get still, get quiet, and get God's sweet Words into my spirit. I like it because I am not trying to swallow large chunks of Scripture trying to devour the Bible in a year as I check off the little boxes in my daily reading guide, but instead I am learning to simply enjoy listening to God as He speaks to my spirit, as He uses His phrases, sometimes even just a word or two to speak life to me. After I hear it in my heart, I sing it back to Him, pray it back to Him, shout it back to Him, and write it back to Him. All of this is my own personal recipe for "chewing the cud," through contemplative biblical meditation.

So when I am together with others, especially for any length of time, I always desire to share how these daily delights are walked out in my personal history with God. But ultimately, it is up to my friends to decide what to do to develop these important times with God and turn them into life practices. The goal has always been to not pass along ideas, even if they are good, but that the student learns and actually begins to do what is shared.

Mentoring is so much more about entering into someone else's journey and honoring the invitation to enter their path. It is far more than just looking over their shoulder for some kind of rote checkbox mentality in which I am the instructor grading their test scores. It is entering into and experiencing the "blow by blow" of their fight and their journey.

It is helping them to experience God for themselves at the highest level. It is showing them how to even be with someone. The questions become endless as we ask what the Father is doing in and through our times together. I am not as curious whether they are doing what I am doing, but rather, what they and the Father are doing because of our times spent together.

In the same way good parenting is about "roots" and "wings," I want them to know what to do, and ultimately to know it by doing it, as the Father teaches them to soar.

The Socratic Approach

Thus, the supreme importance of a Socratic approach of discovery is by asking the right questions. There are no textbooks, no preprinted inventory sheets, or interview packets that will instruct you how to approach your disciple in a highly chaordic way.

There is not a Website or special tried-and-true plan. And to even look to books, or curriculum, or materials is antithetic to the very process of walking alongside someone and enjoying the whole experience of chaordic leadership.

You can start understanding this Jesus-style of asking questions by reading the conversations of Jesus in the Book of John. Nicodemus in John 3, the woman at the well in John 4, the woman caught in the act of adultery in John 8, and Peter in John 21 help us to see that Jesus was not just a great preacher, He was a very effective conversationalist. Whether through prophetic interviews or straight observation, His ability to connect is what He shows us.

In this same way, as we learn to simply be with someone, listening and asking questions, and then responding on an as-needed basis, in that moment we intuitively tap into this back-and-forth chaordic pattern that works for you and those you lead.

The basic Socratic approach of learning to ask the right questions and being with them as the "come alongside cheerleader" is yours to enjoy. And their mutual living in honest response to those moments sets the course in helping them to stay on their personal journey with you.

In Eugene Peterson's *The Message Remix,* he describes David's prayer in Psalms 51:10, where he talks about God creating a new heart and a right spirit in him, as *"shaping a Genesis week from the chaos of my life."*

Larry Crabb challenges us in his classic book *Connecting:*[2]

First, the essence of connection:

- Accepting who we are

- Envisioning who we could be

Second, the affirming exposure:

- Remaining calm when badness is visible

- Keeping confidence that good lies beneath

And, finally, a disruptive exposure:

- Claiming the special opportunities to reveal grace that the difficult content of our hearts provide

This is what mentoring seems to be, entering into someone else's *"Genesis Week"*—entering into his or her season of challenging and even difficult creative beginnings. Mentoring is to actually enter into a relationship with another that is about that person and not you, even if you must walk sad and sticky parts of another's path. The way this is done is by learning to listen to God and to that individual in order to discover where the person is going and how you might cooperate with the journey.

This is a litmus test for who you might be considering for mutual discipleship. Start asking yourself the questions now: "Who in your life do you spend the most time with?" "What relationships do you have that tend to bring up the most questions, and the most interaction about their journey, their life, their dreams, their concerns?" You will discover a direct correlation between their question and answer patterns, and their openness to the concept of journeying with you when your invitation has discipleship questions already built in.

Endnotes

1. Wayne and Clay Jacobsen, *Authentic Relationships* (Grand Rapids, MI: Baker Books, 2003), 104.

2. Larry Crabb, *Connecting* (Nashville, TN: Word Publishing, 1997), 11.

CHAPTER 7

LISTENING TO LEAD

IN THE *COACHING REVOLUTION* by David Logan and John King, this is called "listening for,"[1] which is different than what is called the everyday kind of "listening to." This kind of listening is essential if we intend to lead differently.

A well-known business coach in Logan and King's book was asked how he helped turn around a major division of a Fortune 500 corporation. Without a second of hesitation he said, "I just listened until they told me who they were."[2]

Even in asking certain questions, we need to be careful that we are "listening for," as opposed to asking our professional leading questions, waiting for our preset agenda answers that are again so much about us and not the ones we are with. What is it about their journey and their life that we are being invited to participate with? One of my favorite questions of all time to ask is, "What would you attempt for God, if you knew you couldn't fail?" This, as any good Socratic question, requires far more than a yes or no answer. In fact, this one is a very costly question to ask. It reveals a person's destiny, and could, in fact, alter yours.

It is a very sad commentary that many leaders simply do not listen. Or as someone has said, "Most conversation in our culture is two people waiting for the other person to shut up." Too many of today's lecturing leaders have lost the fine art of listening.

Learning some basic listening skills goes a long way in mentor-to-mentor relationships and makes all the difference in conveying to someone your honor for them and your intent to walk with them. I remember a dear old saint telling me one day after I had preached a sermon on communication in marriage that she looked at it this way: "we have two ears and one mouth," and she insisted, "that means we should do twice as much listening as talking."

With lengthy monologues from the Sunday talk-in-the-box model of the weekend meetings, we have become experts at speaking to, preaching at, and lecturing boldly, and very poor at dialogue, interaction, basic Q & A, and listening for. As a consistently verbose guy, I know I have missed enormous opportunities to be with people just for them, and have a horrible habit of monopolizing the conversations. Wanting so desperately for people to hear what I have to say, I appear to listen only to interrupt them often finishing their sentences, so I can get to my next point. I operate from a lifestyle of content-driven interaction, rather than relationship-discovery.

For all you old Navigator fill-in-the-blanks, purpose-driven-guys, learning to be with someone, learning the art of listening and the character shift of being dream sensitive will take some time. It will begin by leaving your discipleship booklets and printouts at home for a while and learning to live with someone else in listening moments.

Someone recently passed along to me another Sweetism, some fresh thoughts from Leonard Sweet, *"Listen while you can, so you may lead when you must."*[3]

In missionary terms, this is called *contextualizing.* When you consider and discern the ethos of another person, you must choose to enter their context. When you perceive your personal context, your needs, your desires, your values, your personality, even your own biases, prejudices and pet peeves, it helps you to risk entering theirs. All of these form your context, and how you show up in life, and too often determine not only who you are, but what you do. But there are other contexts than just yours.

There is also an eco-context, which includes simple things like the natural world that surrounds you and can so radically affect any conversation—furniture, location, noise level, temperature, season, time of day, other factors in the environmental or ecological context. This is the "where" of your relationship.

This context is particularly significant in the early stages of building the relationship you hope to foster with the one God has called you to walk with. Over time you will learn to experiment with different environmental contexts, whether they become a favorite coffee shop, a walk on the beach, sitting at a certain park bench, or even the more spontaneous e-mails, blogs, and phone calls.

It is simply discerning the components of your surroundings when you meet, and where you meet, what affect they have on the meeting—good or bad.

There is a cultural context that includes the learned behaviors—rules and belief systems that affect our interaction with others. If you come from a culture (foreign or within your own country) where it is considered rude to make long, direct eye contact, you will have to shift your context. If the other person comes from a culture where long, direct eye contact signals trustworthiness, then you will have to cooperate, or at least understand their cultural context to grow in your communication. This is the "who" of your relationship. Different cultures even exhibit a physical context regarding spatial distance, or your proximity to the person you are speaking to.

As you respect these contexts, then come the Socratic questions: Where are you headed in life? Where are you going? Where do you want to go? What are your dreams? How can I and God help you get there?

This means dropping those preset filters and really listening—listening for what they say and the feelings that are behind what they say, not listening for you, but listening for them. This not only involves a fresh way of approaching certain questions, it may even mean discovering your own patterns or bad habits that hinder good conversation. It means learning new ways to speak as well as new ways to listen.

I remember visiting a home for aging seniors early in my pastoral days. I was trying to communicate with a bed-ridden old saint, and as a habit was raising the level of my voice to get his attention. I thought, as most do, that old people who are hard of hearing need you to speak louder to get their attention, which meant I had been talking loud to older people my whole life.

Suddenly, an intern stepped in the door and tapped me on the shoulder. He said as politely as he could, "Not everyone who is hard of hearing needs to be shouted at. Sometimes, if you put your mouth close to their ear, speak softly and enunciate, they will hear you."

Man, what a revelation! It was quite humbling, and at the same time extremely freeing to begin to practice that little communication shift, and what a difference it made. I know I am far from being a listening or communication expert, but I have learned some basic stuff over the years that are helpful and really work.

Another big tool has to do with feedback. Because so much of the communication process is nonverbal, asking the right questions, and endeavoring to make the right assessments about their responses helps convey to them that you are actually listening for who they are.

The Captured Moments

Your interactive responses or your "echo" to their responses and what they have to say can give great dividends. You suddenly feel them lift up physically, get passionate, and get excited about the interaction. It often shows in their eyes, their smile, even their posture shift of leaning forward. They sometimes become louder, get more animated. Suddenly, in the middle of your conversation, their soul gets animated.

Along the way, you can learn to gauge your own meaningful sounds of positive feedback—and they matter. They are not just props. If you fake them just for response, you're busted. In *The*

Coaching Revolution[4] they say that coaches listen in such a way that produces those magic words—duh, aha, wow, and shazam.

These responses happen all of the time when the sounds of discovery are happening with your friend over coffee, on a walk, praying together, or just hanging out and enjoying the coaching/mentoring process. And, as they dream outloud and hear themselves, these sounds even come from deep inside their sense of who they are. They end up discovering all over again how God made them and what He has called them to do.

I have to confess that way too much of my life as a lecturing model leader has been getting people to sign up for my vision, to enroll them in my goals—getting people to affirm my giftings, my ministry, and basically, affirm my stuff. Along the way, I unwittingly shut down, and maybe even killed some other people's dreams at the expense of the tyranny of my own ministry. It is what Graham Cooke says that modern-day Pharisees do; he calls them "dream thieves."

Enrolling people to join my vision, as opposed to empowering them to theirs, has consumed way too much time in my search for my significance. Staffing, denominational monthly reports, weekly team meetings, the stewardship of my vision and my five-year plan have taken the place of really listening for someone else's vision, making room for someone else's dream, and entering someone else's context.

In my early days of desiring transition into a more authentic and organic form of community, I quickly discerned that my addiction to certain corporate practices would invade everything I do and would hinder where I wanted to go relationally.

Of course, I am not stupid. I also know that if I actually ask you about your dreams and you risk telling me what they are, I will have to make a decision about whether I will enter your journey and make that commitment to come alongside to see your dreams fulfilled. So it is risky to really listen; it will cost you.

However, when I do that, when I ask the right questions, and I hear you risking by sharing your dreams, I respond with specific affirmation and some tangible benefits emerge. Most importantly, you begin to believe I am genuinely interested in what interests you, and then the wonderful chaordic journey begins.

Endnotes

1. David Logan and John King, *The Coaching Revolution* (Avon, MA: Adams Media, 2004), 20.

2. Logan and King, 20.

3. Leonard Sweet, *Summoned to Lead* (Grand Rapids, MI: Zondervan, 2004).

4. Logan and King, 14, 15.

CHAPTER 8

DISCIPLING BY DESIGN

DREAM QUESTIONS ARE SO IMPORTANT because they are some of the first insights you get. These pieces of information are crucial in revealing what others think their destiny is. This is revealed through a combination of their own history, their gifts or skill sets, and the dreams that keep coming up in their lives. What you are doing now is mining for and discovering a unique individual's design in God.

The essence of all creation is that it has a Creator. There is no creation without one. There is no design without a Designer. In the same genre that a painting requires a painter, a design requires a designer. To begin to understand our own personal design, we must begin with who designed us, God, the Creator of Heaven and earth.

Yes, any unbalanced preoccupation with you the creation, the creature, without experiencing the revelation of God as the Designer, is the highest form of idolatry. Yes, the Bible warns that some have "*exchanged the truth of God for the lie, and worshiped and served the creature rather than the Creator*" (Rom. 1:25). Yet the same Word of God warns, "*Do not neglect the gift (charisma) that is in you*" (1 Tim. 4:14).

So, for this reason, everything we discover about ourselves must be built on the foundation of what God reveals to us first about His nature and our place in His plan. All biblical truth begins with the truth about God.

A Creative God of Design

We all know about the mystery of the DNA, the uniqueness of snowflakes and fingerprints, even voiceprints and retina scans. So why not recognize the mysterious stamp of every individual God has made in his or her own special personality or persona, bent, gift-mix, and intrinsic value and delight in God?

When you have a basket of apples, oranges, and bananas, what do you have? Do you have a basket of apples? No! Do you have a basket of oranges? No! You have a basket of fruit. And you cannot compare any type of fruit in the fruit basket with another type of fruit. It is apples and oranges.

One of the very first things to be instilled into those we come alongside is to usher them into the experience of their pure value in God, not a measured value in what they do, not a comparative value of what they do as opposed to others, not a meter as to what they can potentially do, but the intrinsic value in who they are in God.

The Value of People

One of the first fruits of a chaordic relationship, where you actually come alongside someone for him or herself, and not for you, is the value system that is created. They feel loved, cared for, and valued, just because you have come alongside, not because you have done anything, or because they have achieved something. They haven't graduated from your discipleship course, they have not yet boasted all over the world about you, their incredible mentor. All they are doing is walking with you, and you with them. But what value that communicates!

The Scriptures carry a revelation that gives us the basis for how we are valued and need to value each other. It is God's value that He has placed on us that gives each of us significance without comparison. If we know and acknowledge this God, this Maker and Designer, we too will value what He values.

Compare the significance or value placed on the people for Cain and his descendants in Genesis 4, with that of Adam's descendants through his son Seth in Genesis 5.

Cain built a city (see 4:17).

- Jabal was good with livestock (see 4:20).

- Jubal was a good musician (see 4:21).

- Tubal-Cain forged tools (see 4:22).

- Finally, Lamech was a crazed murderer (see 4:23,24).

At the end of Chapter 4, everything changes. Genesis 4:26 tells us why: *"Then men began to call on the name of the Lord."*

From that point on, a man's value was based on his significance in God's Creation, not on what he did, not on what he accomplished, or didn't accomplish, not on his gifts or talents, not even his offspring, but his life.

- Adam lived 930 years (see 5:5).

- Seth lived 912 years (see 5:8).

- Enosh lived 905 years (see 5:11).

- Kenan lived 910 years (see 5:14).

- Mahalel lived 895 years (see 5:17).

- Jared lived 962 years (see 5:20).

We are valued simply because God values us. Our value is an intrinsic value. God's endorsement of us shows up in the Book of Beginnings, Genesis. He says about everything He made, "*God saw that it was good*" (Genesis 1:10,12,21,25), but He said specifically of man's creation, "*and indeed it was very good*" (Genesis 1:31).

Nothing shouts value more than a commitment from one person to another to come alongside for the long haul, for that journey to destiny. So first and foremost, then, our walking with others is a walk of love.

When people feel understood and loved, the potential is endless, their destiny sure.

CHAPTER 9

DETAILED DISCIPLESHIP

WHEN WE COME ALONGSIDE to lead someone, the early stages are wisely given to the priority of helping them discover how they as an individual are built, what makes them tick, what are their passions, and what are they designed for. This is not random disciple making. It is your intentional cooperation with the design and the Designer.

As you walk with anyone with a commitment to integrity and loyalty, you will soon discover their gifting, their bent, or what God has designed them for. Some of this will be solidified as you help them discover their passions, their propensities, as well as their weaknesses and failings that quickly become more and more evident as you observe and walk with them.

Much of their design also gets communicated and confirmed by those around them who know them better than you, like their family and friends.

Any attempts to serve God with someone or help him or her find destiny remains mysterious, even harsh, until that specific design is determined. Who you are and what you are called to do are bound together and form a common nexus, a divinely constituted knot that cannot be untied without eroding the nature and purpose of each.

The one always forms the context for the other. Service, or how you serve God, must always be understood against the backdrop of your design, your gifts, or how God has wired you and wants to use you.

So we begin this art of listening and looking for the design this person carries. And in doing so, we can also help warn and protect the person from the distractions and legalistic snares that already exist in Christendom that have for years unduly preoccupied believers, too often keeping them from finding their rest in their God-given design.

Warning #1: Increased Effort Will Not Substitute for Design

God's gifts or designs are the endowments of God for the sole purpose of service and ministry. Effective service is never the product of consecration alone, however sincere and genuine. Effectiveness is more often a carefully crafted use of God's design in you, in conjunction with others whom God has designed around you.

Consecration is vital, and long-term competency in your gifting or design can be linked to faithfulness. But no ministry, regardless of the depth and intensity of your consecration, will sustain itself in the absence of God's cunningly devised strategy based on the utilization of His well-developed gifts in you.

Warning #2: Increased Holiness Will Not Substitute for Design

Too many sincerely committed Christians are wallowing in the mire of despair by claims, which suggest that ineffective ministry is the result of a lack of holiness in their lives. So...

- Back to the mountains

- Back to the deserts

- Back to fasting

- Back to a mind-numbing, heart-wrenching asceticism

- Back to the terrible introversion designed to ferret out every sin

But, they still experience the same ineffectiveness, the same lack of fulfillment, the same lack of joy. All of the holiness, and stripping, and repenting, and continued pursuit of intimacy with God may help you into a greater discernment of your gift, but it will never replace it.

No carpenter can effectively use a saw to pound nails, and no manner of soul-searching and strenuous devotion to duty on the part of the carpenter will make the saw a more effective hammer. A saw is meant to cut boards, not pound nails, and the carpenter is doomed to endless frustration until he finally abandons his efforts to pound nails with a saw and instead concentrates on cutting boards.

The carpenter's faithfulness has already been well established. His only mistake consists of employing a saw for a purpose, that only a hammer is designed to serve. It is not a mistake in zeal or dedication; it is a mistake rooted solely in deficient knowledge. A carpenter who is given a saw, not a hammer, will be effective, fulfilled, and joyful, only in cutting boards, never pounding nails, digging ditches, or installing electrical wire.

The Tension Between Joy and Effectiveness

One of the surest ways to begin to recognize their design is suggest what we already see in them, pushing toward whether or not they have a working knowledge of God's design in them. Here, two things are necessary: One is the "joy" quotient, or what makes them happy, and the second is the "effectiveness" quotient, or what makes us happy.

In other words, it is not enough that someone sees himself or herself doing something, or liking something. The question is, do we also see them doing that, and do we like them doing it?

Another way to ask this of the individual is, "What would you attempt for God if you knew you couldn't fail?" Or a statement that impressed me many years ago, "God is the most glorified in us, when we are the most satisfied in Him."

Functioning in your design and gifting is critical because it is your passion point, it is what moves you, drives you, and delights you. These giftings are who you are all the time. They fit your desires, your likes and dislikes; they are the "you" that God made.

Design Gifts

Considering the three major gift clusters *(Romans 12, 1 Corinthians 12, Ephesians 4)* in the New Testament, I believe the language of the New Testament gives great clues to the fact that concerning the *Motivational Gifts* in *Romans 12,* or what I call *"design gifts,"* each of us have one of these.

I also believe it is clear that the Holy Spirit flows and distributes the *Manifestation Gifts* in *1 Corinthians 12* as He wills in any situation or setting, or as John Wimber, founder of the Vineyard Movement, used to say, concerning the *Spiritual Manifestation Gifts* of *1 Corinthians 12: 8-10, 20-31, "the gifts are frequently understood as given individually and unilaterally to each member of the body. My perception is that we have wrongfully interpreted that text. The emphasis on the gifts is that they are not primarily given to the individual but the whole body.*[1] *"*

And, I believe that God places certain individuals in the Body that are marked as one of the *Ministry Gifts* or *Equipping Gifts* of *Ephesians 4.* These are the influencers of the Body and function best as chaordic teams helping to prepare the Body for its ministry.

My first introduction, like so many other leaders, to what have been called the *Romans 12 Motivational Gifts,* was from Bill Gothard as he popularized them in the 1970s, in his *Institute in Basic Youth Conflicts,* what is now being called, the *Institute in Basic Life Principles.* Many might even conclude that Bill was the guru to this study of *Romans 12*[2].

By my recall I even remember a story passed on of how all seven of these *Romans 12* gifts show up at a dinner party and how they responded to some spilled dessert. On the way in from the kitchen, the servant slips and spills the dessert, with each gift responding, and each response revealing the distinct nature of their individual design motivation:

The prophet points out that she might have been in a hurry. The teacher insists the tray was out of balance with too much dessert on one side. The mercy person has already identified with her embarrassment and reached out to calm her emotions. The encourager has endeavored to free her of her embarrassment by saying this could happen to anyone. The giver has already sent someone out with some funds to purchase another dessert. The server has quickly jumped to retrieve the tray and seat her to calm her down, and finally the facilitator or administrator or leader has directed one to get a broom, another a mop, and help clean up the spilled mess.

Over the years, we have even learned these designs are given to God's people by God as permanent possessions, and knowing what they are can help individuals bridge the gap between their gifting and their occupational choices in life.

Free to Be Who God Made

Helping that person you are walking alongside to discover who they are in God's design is of utmost importance for the journey to be successful. It is the way God gets His glory, and the way the individual gets his delight. Your design gift becomes your basic motivation and causes you to automatically function in a certain way:

- These giftings are the real factors behind your decisions and actions.

- These giftings are indications of the thing you do best.

- They are built into you, and can even be observed in childhood.

- And because one gift gives us only one perspective of the whole, our gift colors what we see.

The Metron of Gifting

The text in Romans 12:6 uses the phrase *"having these gifts,"* which means we have one of these. And then the phrase goes on to add, "having then gifts differing according to the grace that is given us," which implies that yours will be different than someone else's.

It also lets us know in the earlier parts of this text that we all have something in common. We have the *faith* necessary to reveal what these gifts are. So we have *grace* (verse 6) and *faith* (verse 3) to clearly live in these gifts.

Your measure of faith might be seen as the *"determining principle of your tendencies,"* or what we have faith to see in ourselves, what we have faith to do, and the faith that allows us to test ourselves.

It is the stuff behind these consistent propensities that determines how God made us. So somehow this always shows. You and I may have many talents. The person you are walking with could have a wonderful, even a wild world filled with dreams. And the more dream-sensitive you become in your listening and asking certain questions, the more those dreams will be entrusted to you. But ultimately, these continuous actions, dreams, and questions keep showing us our design.

This is who you are, this is the stuff that comes easy to you, and it is your personality, your way of seeing life, your filter, your lens, and thus, your design. You may operate in many of those *manifestation gifts* listed in 1 Corinthians 12. You may even be set as one of those with *ministry gifts* within the matrix of Ephesians 4, but even those gifts will come from your base, your design gift.

For example, I learned many years ago that I am a Romans 12 exhorter who also tends to flow the easiest in the 1 Corinthians 12 vocal gifts of words of knowledge, words of wisdom and prophecy, along with healing and faith. I also function as an apostolic influence in my equipping gift of Ephesians 4.

We do go through seasons of "gift blindness," when we simply don't know, and when we are first exposed to these principles we often go through a season of "gift confusion" or "gift comparison." This is normal, but as we walk this out, particularly with others who echo what they see, things become clearer, and tremendous rest, safety, and purpose and clarity come to our lives.

Because, as the Scripture shares, we all have *"been dealt a measure of faith,"* according to Romans 12:3. Strong's concordance 3358, calls this "faith," "metron." So this can be the meter, or measure, or metron of how your faith works in expressing that specific motivation.[3] This helps furnish a testing ground for a normative standard of someone's respective endowments and functions. In other words, it is measurable. In whatever gift you function, you will receive a direct benefit in keeping with that gifting as you use it. You will see it, and others will see it. It is measurable.

In other words, this is what you do, how you react, and thus who you are, and we see it again and again. For more help in assisting your friend into his or her clear understanding of God's design in them, visit Bill Gothard's Website, originally the *Institute in Basic Youth Conflicts*, now called the *Institute in Basic Life Principles.*[4]

This is not everything you are going to learn about each other as you walk together; time will determine the longevity of your relationship, and over a period of time your commitment will reveal what information will come out of your walking together into your chaordic relationship and destiny. But helping someone discover his or her design gift and its impact on that person's future is a very important place to begin.

Your goal is to find the unique individual that God has called you to walk with, not to become the ventriloquist for that person's gifting. He or she is not called to be your latest clone. Your goal is to enjoy the surprise and delight with others as they make the discovery of who they are, and what God has called them to be, so you get to value them, bless them, and walk with them in their design.

Endnotes

1. John Wimber, *The Way In is the Way On* (Atlanta, GA: Ampelon Publishing, 2006), 226.

2. Rick Walston, *Unraveling the Mystery of the Motivational Gifts* (Fairfax, VA: Xulon Press, 2002), 22.

3, Strong's Concordance, 3358.

4. http://www.iblp.org/iblp/.

CHAPTER 10

CHAORDIC GROUPS

AS WE HAVE ALREADY STATED, life transformation will come best through the one-on-one context of dream weaving and journeying, and as well will come through your chaordic leadership within small groups. Both are necessary in this new way of leading, this new way of "doing church."

In both cases we come alongside others. We don't lead over them using heavily formatted agendas; but we do listen to them and live life together. In both cases, this mutual mentoring takes place as the atmosphere is full of face time, dialogue, Q & A, interaction, and giving and taking when it comes to communication.

These chaordic small groups are not your classic home groups. They are not your typical cell groups, not small group Bible studies, not even traditional house churches. They are basically interactive laboratories that help lead to the exploration. They are dream teams, think tanks, farm leagues, where people discover who they are and are launched into their present-future.

They are really more like birthday parties, small tribes getting together to celebrate life and uniqueness. There is a lot of talking, a lot of listening, a lot of laughing, and a lot of crying. And they are consistent gatherings where all share their gifts, all pray, all eat, all bless, and all encourage one another.

Even the leader is more like a player-coach who shares in the life of the group, and is served as often as he serves. They are what the Filipinos call *barkada,* or a circle of friends who live as family. And every time they get together, they *salo-salo,* or share-share.

Larger Chaordic Meetings

A note about larger meetings: There is a chaordic dynamic or rhythm that can manifest in the larger gatherings that so fills today's church landscape. When meetings are designed around the mutual edification of the saints and provide a setting for individuals to find and experiment with their gift-mix and passion-mix, larger meetings can help in the long run. These gatherings can be to both stimulate and motivate the army of God for advance if they have not fallen prey to the self-serving of the limited vision and programming of an elite and limited survival staff.

Effective large meetings give adequate "sacred space" for people to encounter the mysteries of God, and then identify with others who, with like passion, can help by launching their corporate quest with deep significance and strategy. These larger meetings can be a unique genesis for taking key leaders who are comfortable enough in their own skin and helping them to make room for the destiny of many others to their next level. Sometimes larger gatherings can provide the venue to connect clusters that then strategize and ignite each other for gift-based service and gift-based outreach. When that happens, it can help fulfill the dream that "the meeting place is the mentoring place for the marketplace."

Not More Meetings, But Actual Meeting

The biggest thing about chaordic life is in the living, not just the meeting or gathering, but the full reality of the lives that meet together, and what that produces and releases in the same way two people walk together.

When a group gathers often enough, especially in an environment of affirming each other by listening and caring, you might visit one of these groups and cannot initially discern who is leading. Living in an effective chaordic group, one cannot quickly find the leader, and could be prone to question whether there even is one.

These chaordic groups are basically spirit-led and self-led. And given the gift of an effective facilitating-leader with the belief in the fully released priesthood of all believers, everyone helps facilitate less or more—and most of the time, less is more. Another way to say this is that these groups are leader-led and need-driven. And because the goal is the honoring participation of all believers, everyone gets to lead.

When some young people were asked about the part of their weekly church gathering that they most looked forward to, they all agreed that it was the meal after the meeting that was the most anticipated. This little survey and its results pose a very controversial reality in the emphasis we make on our institutional meetings. Could it be that with all of our work and rehearsal and planning of our weekend lecture-driven church meetings, we could be missing the point of church?

Even our battles over styles of worship, types of meetings, and liturgical forms at the end of the equation don't really seem to matter, because the issue isn't whether our worship or liturgy is Beatles, Bach or the Beach Boys. The question seems to be, do people actually connect? Do they feel loved? Do they feel heard? Do they feel that church is the intertwining of their lives together in God, or have they accepted the meetings as merely another distribution of information that someone else deems very important for them to endure?

Looking for Fellowships of the Heart

The real primal cry of believers is what John Eldredge describes in his book, *Waking the Dead,*[1] as our need of and desperate search for true community and authentic fellowship. We are after "fellowships of the heart." We know in theory that we are all part of a great company of believers or, as the Nicene Creed calls it, the "holy catholic" or "universal church," yet we all tend to function best in little platoons, in smaller companies of friends that are our intimate "allies of the heart."

Years ago, the title of a book caught my eye. I never read it, but its message was clear. *Crowded Pews and Lonely People* reminded me of the reality that meetings do not guarantee true community, much like beautiful weddings do not guarantee successful marriages.

Like many, I have come to the conclusion that this kind of true community, of real connectedness, is hard work. I think the reason why so many believers remain warehoused in our weekend gatherings is because getting to know one another takes too much time, too much energy, and way too much effort.

After all, if I meet with a small group of believers that are openly sharing their lives together, I can no longer plead ignorance to the plight and journey of others. If I hang around you long enough, you just may leak some parts of your daily struggles that suck me into offering my prayers, and partnership with you in your journey. I may have to actually show up and do those "one another's," with you, as mentioned in the Scriptures.

Our large, detached meetings feed the disease of isolation that has so predominantly marked church as we know it. And because loneliness is not an isolation of space, but an isolation of spirit, being surrounded by gobs of people worshiping, singing, "doing church" doesn't mean community is actually happening. Even joining with others in meetings through prayer and sharing does not guarantee you really have connected with those people in a way that meets your true fellowship needs.

Somewhere on your journey, you are looking for real faces in your fellowship. Without them, you are missing what real fellowship really looks like.

Chaordic groups are not your heavily formatted weekly studies with 30 minutes of this, followed by 20 minutes of that, all neat and tidy. They are not extensions of the program-mentality of weekend flagship church. They are chaordic, even messy, as you listen to the buzz, the laughter, the chatter, and the shocking stories, the debates and disagreements. This whole journey speaks of people talking, talking, talking, and eating, and laughing, and crying, and shouting, and hurting, and praying, and even silence and waiting.

The group ends up becoming sometimes as simple as an extended meal with God-sightings and life sharing. The only thing formatted might be a "food theme" for the potluck. Most of what really happens in these meetings cannot be scripted. It is spontaneous, interactive, interruptive, and "divinely chaotic," as normally isolated individuals are looking for points of connection, support, encouragement, prayer, and an overall sense of deep belonging.

We Are All Looking for Something

Looking for Faces of Faith

Whether it is sharing God-sightings in your life, your most recent answers to prayer, or the latest revelation of God in your personal time with the Father, if you don't have people to hear these things and get excited about them with you, this Christian walk lacks bounce and sense of lift. Even the greatest episodes in your life lose their flavor quickly unless you get to share these stories with others.

In the little book *"How Full Is Your Bucket?"* by Tom Rath and Donald Clifton, Tom describes what his grandfather Don defines as the core of *positive psychology* by focusing on what is right with people.[2]

It is called the Theory of the Dipper and the Bucket:

Each of us has an invisible bucket. It is constantly emptied or filled, depending on what others say or do to us. When our bucket is full, we fell great. When it's empty, we feel awful. Each of us has an invisible dipper. When we use that dipper to fill other people's buckets—by saying or doing thing to increase their positive emotions—we also fill our own bucket. But when we use that dipper to dip from others' buckets—by saying or doing things that decrease their positive emotions—we diminish ourselves."

The biblical principle is called *mutual edification,* which has been described as the premiere reason the Early Church gathered. They did not meet for worship, teaching, evangelism, or even fellowship, but something deeper, something highly intentional. They met for the consistent "building up" of one another and "filling each others' buckets."

Looking for Faces of Failure

This face must be revealed and risked as we are willing to reveal to others who we "are not." This one requires a lot of trust and a lot of work. It asks looming questions: "Who do I share my battles with?" "Who do I trust them with?" Knowing my successes or my feats of faith are not enough. "Who do I open up to about my fears, my failures, and my faults?"

Regular times of meeting with one another as well as regular times of praying for one another, regular times of opening up, of confession, of admission, and of vulnerability take a real commitment to the time that strong relationships require. Openness breeds openness, honesty breeds honesty, and hiding breeds hiding.

One of the reasons fear becomes such a force in our lives is that it flourishes in the dark, the darkness of simply fighting your fears by yourself. It is amazing how the very act of speaking your fears turns on the lights, and breaks you out of dark places.

You find out a lot of things when you speak your fears, your faults, and your failures. You realize you are not actually alone at all. You find out they are common, consistent, and conspicuous in other believers' lives as well. And the art of listening to other brothers and sisters helps you fight them together and win. Like someone said, we need a place to share both our "wows and our wars."

Looking for Faces of Fun

You do need other faces to share your faith, your fears, failures, and faults. But something else needs to be incorporated in this journey. You have to have people to smile and laugh with. Some of the fellowships of people I have traveled with over the years have felt too much like an exhausting triathlon rather than the sensation of floating down a refreshing stream in a big ole' inner tube with a few friends, just enjoying the ride.

Many of my Christian friends (especially pastors) haven't a clue about having fun. Everything is about the latest, greatest, and most serious new intercessory assignment, the current prophetic temperature of the times, or the leader's infatuation with giftings and callings to be lethal weapons in the latest warfare scrimmages. Our times together feel more like war room strategy sessions for the final phases of the cosmic battle than a night at the Comedy Store with friends.

I know these are the last days. I know times are tough, and very serious, and I know we have work to do, but come on, lighten up. If I recall correctly, we have all read the last page of the book, and we win. For years, God has been after me to help me enjoy my life and not take myself so seriously.

I think it is especially true of the next generation that they are looking for dependable and meaningful relationships that are based on friendships and socializing, a way of being together that feels altogether like hanging out at the mall or having pizza, rather than the newest prophetic dissection of the evening news.

Looking for Faces of the Future

There is a specific part of your journey that must be traveled alone, or as M. Scott Peck called it, *The Road Less Traveled,* and there also is a significant part of your journey that will only be discerned, mapped out and discovered as it is traveled with a few select fellow travelers.

In the same way you make room for God through solitude in your life, you have to invite a certain community into your journey by sharing your dreams, your aspirations, and even the ideas about what your future might look like.

Part of your fellowship walk must include a "dream team," or people who know where you want to go. These teams must be made up of people that not only believe in God but also believe in you. They are not "dream thieves," they are your own personal "dream team." These are people who celebrate you.

So what does your fellowship life look like? I am not talking about how many meetings you are attending weekly. Are you walking with true allies of the heart? Do you have people in your life that you feel free enough to share your adventures and your faults with? People who really care for you and have your back?

Do you have people who cry with you when you are crying? Do you have people who laugh with you when you are laughing? When was the last time you met with your friends and laughed so hard your sides hurt for days?

Do you have people in your life with which you have risked the stewardship of your dreams? And are their people in your life actually committed to helping you get to where you are going? True friends are there for the best of days and the worst of days, and all of the days in between.

When you willingly enter someone else's chaos in a small group, it is also an invitation for them to enter into yours. In that sense, we all need more chaordic relationships.

Endnotes

1. John Eldredge, *Waking the Dead* (Nashville, TN: Thomas Nelson, 2003), 185.

2. Tom Rath and Donald Clifton, *How Full Is Your Bucket?* (New York, NY: Gallup Press, 2004), 15.

CHAPTER 11

CHAORDIC OR CHAOTIC?

THIS QUESTION RELATES to the simple understanding of the effect of the amount of people regularly meeting in a small group that ultimately determine whether it will be congruent with what we call a small chaordic group, or something larger with a different dynamic.

This is often a little trickier than one thinks. You might be thinking, "If the goal is just to get a bunch of people together and for the leader to help facilitate a lot of talking and interaction, what could possible go wrong?"

The Size and the Outcome

For one thing, I have experienced that the size of these groups is too critical to what they become. Some groups feel chaotic and not chaordic, simply because we have let them get too large, and when that happens they do not present the best vehicle, or the best venue, for meaningful sharing and meaningful connecting.

So, when talking about counting, I am not talking about some new numerology or strange set of numerics, but more basically what happens when certain numbers of people gather. This is not science, and I am not pretending to be some kind of group dynamics expert, but it has seemed to me, after many years of observation and participation with different sized groups, that when they gather they end up with certain sets of dynamics, often directly determined by their size, whether by design or default.

And if we care deeply about a new kind of lifestyle of sharing when we get together, I think we need to honor that chaordic value and watch with great discernment the size of the meeting. Chaordic living means lots of one-on-one walking and lots of small-group talking.

Because I believe so strongly in the interactive qualities of these groups, I end the book with a pretty exhaustive list of questions: questions of trivia, questions of fun, questions of memories that can keep this talking thing going. Sometimes just using a question or two occasionally, or whenever the group bogs down, really helps. The group can get jump-started by listening to each other and praying for each as we ask the right questions, and even help us to enjoy the journey with others.

Much of what I have written in the last two decades about "doing church differently" has been directly related to an experimental approach of the gathering of believers around the numbers laid out in Exodus 18:21. Jethro gave counsel to his son-in-law, Moses, to place leaders over different sized groups of 10, 50, 100, and 1,000 for more efficient administration of Israel.[1]

It does seem that numbers or size matters when it comes to both life and Scripture. I also will be the first to confess there are problems in the past with "why" we counted people. Unfortunately, like David numbering Israel, we can get in trouble when we count heads for the wrong reasons.

Sadly, the "numbers game" of today's churches has woefully become nothing but a great burden placed on the shoulders of too many church leaders. Too often, it artificially affects the core of the leader's identity, simply by the "how manys" of the weekend gatherings. In this sad scenario, the counting of "nickels" and "noses," or "budgets, buildings, and bodies," has both crushed and/or deified way too many leaders in their feeble attempts of obedience to God.

There always seems to be someone else who ends up with better stats or better numbers, with many of the marketing "bean counters" of our day overready to compare those numbers or results. Besides, these are the pulpit heroes we platform—the largest church, the largest Sunday school, the biggest ministry, the most TV or radio stations.

Setting numbers, or leveraging plateaus, or marketing thresholds and lids, or ceilings that get used to define someone's success or lack thereof, and that ultimately scar people's identity and their sense of worth, rather than their gifting and calling, can be devastating. So whether it is megachurch or microchurch, basing a quantum expectation on the gatherings of God's people for the wrong reasons has proven to bring unrealistic expectations and misses the whole adventure of what is happening in a certain-sized group.

I am after more of a sane study of numbers that impact effective simple group dynamics, and do not stem from a need for competition, but an appreciation of the outcomes of these natural dynamics that come when groups of a specific size gather.

Numbers and Pictures in Scripture

Many know the prophetic implications of the many often-quoted numbers in the Bible. Examples include 3 and the Trinity; 7 and the days of Creation or the Feasts of Israel; 12 and the Tribes of Israel, the disciples of Jesus, or the gates of Jerusalem; 50 for Pentecost or the Year of Jubilee.

When I was a young denominational pastor, you needed 25 attendees to be a chartered church, and years later I would go to a conference specifically targeted to "Breaking the 200 Barrier." The premise of this conference was that when around 200 people attended the church meetings on a regular basis, a pastor needed to shift from the "shepherd" model to the "rancher" model, where he worked through other designated key leaders.

The New Testament refers many times to the different-sized gatherings around Jesus. John the Beloved, the first, Peter, James, and John, the 3, the 12 disciples and the apostles. Jesus sent out the 70, or 72, two by two in Luke 10:1, the 120 gathered in the Upper Room when the Holy Spirit fell at Pentecost in Acts 2.

Jesus did not necessarily use words like "bunch," "crowd," "gang," or "team," but often gave specific and definite connections to numbers. Even in His feeding of the 5,000 men plus the women and children with five loaves and two fishes, in Mark 6:40, He requested that they sit in groups of 50 and 100. In the chapter on

"Lost Things" in Luke 15, Jesus, when speaking of a shepherd, specified that this shepherd did not lead an ambiguously sized flock of any size but a specific flock of 100 (see Luke 15:4).

Numbers Count

For example, a group of two can be tremendously creative (as in parents), but requires deep commitment by both parties and could become polarized. Notably, often the difficulty of a two-person business partnership is compared to that of a marriage, yet a group of three is not always stable, as one person can feel left out, or one person can control the others by being the "split" vote.

Consensus is that at five the feeling of "team" really starts. At five to eight people, you can have a meeting where everyone can speak out and everyone feels empowered.

But also note that on your way to a larger group, there can be a breakdown with not enough time or attention given to everyone. The risk is that things will become either too noisy, too boring, too long, or some combination thereof.

I have actually enjoyed some great times with groups between seven to ten. It's fairly easy for us to see and agree that a dinner party starts to break down somewhere above seven or eight people, as do some tabletop and other group games.

It is interesting to note that recent church planting movement stats from India indicate that a house church there consists of an average of six baptized believers. This does not include who all may be attending or wanting to attend the specific house church, but does indicate what constitutes a core group for that house church.

As Goes the Size so Goes the Dynamics

When asked about the optimum or perfect size for a small group the counsel really varies. Most would consider a small group anywhere between 7 and 16, with most noting 12 as optimum. And sometimes the size and location, or size of the group and the size of the room, are directly related. In leading a small group in a medical office, 8 to 10 seemed bests for me, while for a small discussion group in a public coffee shop, 5 or 6 seemed to work best.

It has been noted that when groups drop below 6, the diversity in personalities usually is not sufficient to achieve depth in personal growth. And of course you could meet with 4 and still be a small group. Getting much smaller than that is more of an investment in a friendship relationship.[2]

Small-group difficulties usually start somewhere between 9 to 12 people in a group. I read years ago that when 12 started attending regularly, one or two stop talking, and when more than 12 try to regularly attend, one or two stop coming on a consistent basis. As you grow past 12, it seems you must start specializing in a different style of communication, which often becomes direct questions and reports from certain individuals, usually prompted by a leader.

I have often felt the best-sized group for this constant chaordic interaction is close to the first-sized, or the smaller-sized group that Jethro offered Moses in Exodus 18:21: the ten group.

Groups of Ten

According to British author Antony Jay, there are centuries of evidence to support the idea that small groups are the most efficient. In *The Corporation Man*, he talks about how humans have worked in small groups, usually 5 to 15 people, as hunters and farmers for hundreds of generations. The ideal group size is a *ten-group*.

He found the most efficient to be organized in groups of eight to fourteen people, which he came to call "ten-groups," each group free to find its own way toward a target set for it within the general objects.[3]

If any group grows larger than what is consistently considered a small group, becomes more challenging to administrate, and looses its functionality, its chemistry, the new size forces not only an adjustment to leader monologue by the elite few, it struggles with the dialogue portion of the meeting where the intent is that each believer has a right to participate (see 1 Corinthians 14:26), and thus ceases being an effective chaordic small group.

Sometimes, despite the ideal numbers, one or two dominant figures can sway the group. If it's a smaller number of seven or fewer, you may have better inclusive personal interaction, and get more of a consensus or an agreement outcome. When these smaller groups move toward larger groups, the multiple gift-expressed experience happens rather than the consistent sharing of personal and intimate information. Sometimes it is the season, dynamics, chemistry, willingness to open up, desire to care, and all of the above that affect the flow and freedom in a small group. It is really not science but requires the facilitator to discern, keep his eyes and ears open, and see what is happening.

It seems that in the larger groups, people are very strongly influenced by the dominant speakers. In other words, people's opinions tend to go with the dominant ones and not with the person they spoke with or interacted with next to them in the discussion.

However, in the smaller groups, you get quite the opposite result. It has been discovered that dominant speakers have no greater impact than anyone else in the smaller groupings. What seems to determine what people come away with in terms of their changes in attitudes and shifts in beliefs comes from the people they actually interacted with during the discussion. And this is exactly what we expect and enjoy from the smaller group, and the kind of discussion process it fosters. Get five to nine people engaged around an open meal, and somehow talking with your mouths full seems to be the norm.

Whatever the Size

So, when we begin to witness certain things happening with certain numbers, the result is often better management and preparation rather than the discouragement of certain sizes, particularly smaller ones.

In a culture stung with the marketing ego that "bigger is better," we must always be cautious as to why we "count" certain things. Again, numbers are not to be used against one another, but in the model of Jesus and Scripture, the truth is that we can better steward what is happening relationally when the group is the right size and we become aware of the shifts and changes that can occur in order to accommodate different-sized groupings and thus different dynamics.

Jesus comes along and busts all of the so-called experts with His admonition and prayer that when it comes to Jesus and the Father, He prays that we would be *one* (see John 17), and promises that where two or three are gathered together in His name, He is in the middle.

So numbers do count. They just need to count for the right reason.

Preparation for a Chaordic Meeting

Finally, size really does matter when you consider the purpose of the meeting: the mutual edifying, stimulating, and building up of one another and how everyone needs to come prepared for that. In Hebrews 10:24, it says that we are to "consider" the gathering, and those we will be gathering with so that love and good works can be encouraged. I call this "preconsidering."

I think this can only happen successfully when I meet with the same group of a certain number of individuals on a common, regular basis, in order to get real good at this "think ahead" about the meeting, and "preconsidering" what I am to bring and to whom I am to bring those things. So we have to keep asking the questions of each group as to whether the size is affecting the group negatively or positively.

Thinking consciously before the meeting, even days before, during the week pray about certain individuals in the group and try to see what you can bring to the meeting and to those individuals to cause them to be pressed to love and good works. This is preparation for everyone coming to that group. This preconsidering happens best when the meeting is kept the proper size and led for the proper purpose of mutual edification.

If I am meeting with the same people and encouraged to speak into their lives on a regular basis, this will drastically affect how I come to that meeting, how I show up at that meeting, how I pray for the meeting, give myself to that meeting and what that meeting becomes.

Endnotes

1. Graham Cooke and Gary Goodell, *Permission to Do Church Differently in the 21st Century* (Shippensburg, PA: Destiny Image Publishers, 2005), 110.

2. http://www.community4me.com/faq_smallgrp.html.

3. http://37signals.com/svn/posts/995-if-youre-working-in-a-big-group-youre-fighting-human-nature.

CHAPTER 12

KEEPING SMALL GROUPS CHAORDIC

IT WORKS LIKE THIS. In looking at an old anyone/everyone principle, whenever everyone in the small group can no longer do what any individual can do in the small group, the dynamic automatically shifts.

So, if you consistently bring a component into a small group that does not allow for the full potential participation by everyone in that small group, you are no longer honoring this dynamic of a chaordic small group, and that group is destined to become something else.

Again, a chaordic small group is built around the idea that in any given meeting everyone has the full potential to openly share their journey and others in the group can get actually engaged in the process.

We have all experienced that, when you suddenly have a batch of unexpected guests show up at your small group, you quickly notice the rest of the group is no longer as talkative or participative.

Without even planning on it, the group automatically has shifted to a different dynamic with only the few outspoken ones sharing, and the normal free-flow interaction of the group gets detoured, with the group usually having to revert to a Q & A format or even direct lecture with much fewer responses from all of the individuals as the trust that has been built over the weeks lessens with this new batch of visitors.

Far bigger and more predictable than our lofty ideas or thoughts, it is about this law or principle of group dynamics. Because of the size, ultimately the group itself decides what it will look like. And because the small group is all about the potential priesthood of all believers, not just the priesthood of the preachers, or the priesthood of the worship leaders, or the priesthood of the most outspoken and gregarious, these numbers and shifts cannot be ignored.

Unfortunately, we are all too well churched, and for too many years we have catered to this habit of adopting large-group components into our small-group meetings. This habit must stop. We simply thought that these things would make it more meaningful and rich, even though the group was smaller, or we simply missed the elements that work well and are perfectly designed for our larger celebration times.

But much of the repetition of these components or elements is based simply on our old traditions, habits, and adapted styles of leadership. Too often, we do not realize that these large-group components and our addictions to them can, in fact, abort the very group dynamic we are longing for in the smaller group.

For example, for years we formatted the whole small-group meeting with specific individuals leading worship, (smaller instrument-led), or even a controlled check-in time that allowed a little token sharing and participation, all pointing to the individual assigned to share the Word with us that night. Again, our old mental map or old tape is leading from or leading over.

So, is that a small group? Not really. It's more like just a smaller amount of people in a different geographical setting, while we continue to superimpose components typical to a large meeting onto the small group. We have just changed the address. The results? Just okay, with a little more intimacy, a lot more coffee, a more casual seating arrangement, even closer access to the bathroom, but not really the honoring of the dynamics of small groups, more like mini-church than a priesthood of believers chaordic meeting.

What is it in a small group in which everyone can consistently participate? Simple, the category usually falls into eating, talking, and listening, with the goal of everyone being potentially able to experience mutual edification. If we have someone come to the meeting with preset components, then those very components become the agenda for the meeting and can even end up preventing others from the free flow of spontaneous interaction and participation so precious to a small band of believers. Canned, repetitive, predictable components can simply kill a small group, even religious ones.

Losing Chaordic Principles

For example, as previously stated, nothing seems to affect the "anyone/everyone principle" of a small group any quicker than how one or two specified individuals lead worship. The thought is that every gathering of believers, large or small, needs to spend time in songs and musical worship. But this whole approach has to be better thought through, with serious consideration to what actually defines true biblical worship.

Some of our addiction to certain cultural styles of contemporary worship are simply because we are a church gathering culture that has not developed a personal history with God, nor have we developed true holistic relationships with others. Instead, we tend to use worship, or at least worship through songs and music, in a corporate vacuum, even in a small group.

So be careful. If you ask a musician to bring his or her guitar to the small, intimate group, and ask them to consistently lead worship, you may run the risk of modeling something that you really don't want to reproduce. Simply put, that worship can only come out of certain musician(s) or out of certain sounds or songs rather than the potential songs or sounds that spontaneously can come out of one or more or all of the individuals in the group.

When the instrument of one individual and the sounds that one person produces become the sole means of what we call worship, then something stops. Unfortunately, the guitar will become the new pulpit, and the four song sheets on the floor in front of that guitar player will become the new agenda or liturgy or curriculum for the group. And rather than the group being the agenda, the group bringing the sounds of worship, we now all watch the one gift, the one expression, and possibly miss the serendipitous orchestra that God could have led that night.

Trust me. Sounds of worship will come, music will come, and poems will come, maybe riddles will come, maybe stories will come, as well as spontaneous prayers, and freely shared God-sightings. Lots of laughter will be heard, mingled with many tears, and the joyful affirmation of one another. The passing around of the dessert will come, along with the passing of the babies from one person to another, and even the passing of the bread and the cup and so many other creative things out of which God gets pleasure.

These forms and sounds and expressions must be allowed to come out of the group, as everyone continues to be allowed to freely participate as any one individual in that group.

Maybe we need to lower the bar of our expectation of certain music talent and gifting. It seems that God likes what comes from the heart, not just from the art. We don't have to hire or coordinate the professional musician for the house gig; God likes noise, joyful noise, even if it does not always please our musical palette. If we want to honor the dynamics of a small group, let's put up with people's attempts at grunts and groans, and whistles and hums.

Throw a bunch of kids' noisemakers on the table in the middle of the meal and see what comes up. Or hand everyone some pots and pans and spoons. You may drive the neighbors crazy, but it just may please the Father. Or simply make room to host a not-so-polished voice being lifted up a cappella from one of the regular brothers or sisters at the table.

Keeping It Small

A small group can gather easily on a regular basis. Most of the time weekly seems best. That small group can easily fit into a house or even small apartment, and can often fit around a table, or make a circle in the living room.

In this group, the goal is that everyone brings something, so potluck can become the starting point by becoming a prophetic act. Your casserole is how you show up at the beginning of the meeting. Everyone needs to eat, even the kids, who sometimes make the group larger than ten, but they also can function for the most part in another room with their videos, their homework and their laptops. And these little guys are great at all kinds of multi-tasking as they migrate in and out of the adult group. In fact, watch! The kids will invite themselves into a group that laughs, tells stories, interrupts, and enjoys eating together.

The litmus test still stands. When anyone or everyone in the group can no longer do what anyone else in the group is doing, the group dynamic shifts. In all of our doing of meetings, let's try to do this one kind of meeting well.

For many years I have studied and experimented with the group sized counsel that Jethro gave Moses in Exodus 18:21. In Jethro's list, this smaller group of 10 seems like a good prototype for New Testament Church life. In this sized group, the individual gets focused on, and this is also a perfect-sized group for a common meal (see I Corinthians 11), finding Christ, sharing your lives together within this meal, doing it often, and with gladness and simplicity of life, as mentioned in Acts 2. Kind of like the original Happy Meal.

Worship in this small group can be rewriting a couple verses of everyone's favorite Psalm and reading it as worship to God. This can come through sharing passages of Scripture that address a certain theme. Worship can be the individual members of the group sharing an attribute of God that puzzles or mystifies them. We can ask different individuals to share their "life stories" over a series of weeks. Worship can be highly creative without feeling like canned components.

But again, the goal of these groups is walking in each other's shoes, not just learning the latest worship Top 10.

As the groups grow, there is an increased depth and a deeper reach into one another that sets the tone for the gathering greater than anything on an agenda. No heavy formatting necessary, so leave your planned, printed scripts at home. Life is the agenda, and chaos is welcome, with all of the sounds, the interruptions, the surprises, the emoting, and the enjoying. It is chaordic, and it is not only you as the leader modeling coming alongside, but everyone else coming alongside each other as well.

CHAPTER 13

HOW RELATIONSHIPS AND SMALL GROUPS DEVELOP

NOTICE WE DIDN'T SAY, "GROW"—that confuses us again with the Western Church and its preoccupation with size. We have already addressed the size issue but all know that groups, like children and families, have stages of life that they automatically process through in order to grow. Of course, this is growing deeper rather than growing larger. And, of course, the leader's task during this process is to not hinder it, not to push it, and at the same time help people stay on track when they are in a certain process.

Take Me Out to the Ballgame

Lyman Coleman, known for his great influence during the early Serendipity Movement within the Catholic Church, taught that the group process was like playing baseball.[1] Using the bases on the baseball diamond as stages, he gave us language for small group life and the processes or stages that a group passes or cycles through.

Picture the baseball diamond with home plate being the goal of "in-depth Christian community" for a small group. It is the goal at which we are seeking to arrive in the group experience.

In the New Testament, the word *koinonia* is used to express a marriage-like relationship with one another in which there is total openness and freedom to be you. A dynamic where you can share with each other your pains and sorrows as well as your hopes and dreams without fear of condemnation, continually learning how to support each other in love.

Group dynamics can be defined as "the life and growth of the group and of the individuals who attend." The following elements are essential to an effective and healthy small group environment:

First Base/Information

As the rules of baseball dictate, to get to home plate you have to go around the bases, which is another way of saying there is a process to becoming a group. First base in this process might be called history giving.

In this first phase, the members of a group need to take the time to tell about themselves. You need to share:

- *Your past:* Where you came from, your background, something about your family relationships, good times, hard times, your childhood dreams and aspirations, the significant people in your life, your religious roots and your spiritual pilgrimage up to the present

- *Your present:* Where you are right now, your job, your hobbies, what concerns you, what bugs you, what you do for kicks, what keeps you up at night, where you are right now in your faith, and what the growing edge is in your spiritual life and what you need to work on

- *Your future:* Where you want to be five years from now, the scary things you would like to try, and what you feel God is telling you to do

It takes a long time for each member to give this kind of information, but it is absolutely crucial if your small group is really going to become a healing community. The more information you collect, the more you will be able to minister to each other when you get to the deeper levels of group experience. In the early days of serendipity groups many groups began by asking what was called the famous "Quaker questions." Where did you spend your childhood? What was the warmest room in your house? When did you first experience God as more than just a word?

All of this is the wonderful long process of knowing one another and learning to really love the ones you really know.

In principle, it means that in the early stages of your group you will dedicate large chunks of time, even entire meetings, to hearing one another's life story. There is always a lot of talking in small groups, which is what makes them small groups. But in these early stages it is important that people open up and talk about themselves.

You can set aside night after night in these early meetings for someone to tell the group his or her life story. That person can use art, drama, albums, pictures, video, being as creative as they want to be to tell their story, their history. When new people come into the group, give them their time to tell their story.

Again, there is a section at the end of the book with a lot of questions you can mix and match, maybe two to four at a time, that will help people talk about themselves—about what might be called the trivia of their lives, which actually assists the first stage or first base to move the group along.

Second Base/Affirmation

After lots of meaningful times of history giving, the group will almost automatically go on to second base. Let the members of the group respond to each other. In "affirmation," you "enable" each other by pointing out the positive traits you have observed. Then, in the atmosphere of warmth and affirmation, each person shares the things that he would like to change about himself.

In a parable, this might be termed the process of "kissing the frog" resulting in the frog pointing out his own wart. In a sense, affirmation is the process by which we can do for each other what Jesus Christ did for Simon (the vacillating neurotic) when He said, *"Simon, you shall be called Peter, a rock"* (John 1:42). This process will happen as the group grows and allow the group members to recognize positive strengths in each other, and to speak them out in encouragement and affirmation.

Do some activities that point to the dynamic of tying together a diverse group into a group where individuality and unity is sensed. One activity is called "spinning a yarn," where a ball of yarn is passed to an individual. As each person catches the ball of yarn, he or she, in turn, rolls the ball of yarn to another and gives an observation, compliment, or affirmation to the one they pass the yarn ball to. By the time you are through with this exercise, you will have created a web of yarn as it reaches across the room giving a visible lesson of the groups being connected to each other.

Third Base/Participation

In the atmosphere of warmth and acceptance that has been created in the affirmation phase, you move on. The members of the group have been released to a new and deeper level of sharing, based on mutual love and trust. Third base looks much like first base, with each person sharing more information, but this time the information is far more personal: where they are hurting at the moment; where they need to grow in their relationships with their spouse, their children; where they need to be healed; where they need the ministry of Jesus right now, etc.

If you had asked these kinds of questions during the first sessions, you would have scared everyone away and probably killed your group. Remember, you just don't usually talk about your needs to strangers. However, when you have established a trust and confidence in each other, it is only natural to share these things. In fact, if these areas are kept hidden from each other, the group will spiritually die because you would be robbed of one of its basic purposes for existence, that is to become a healing community where the Holy Spirit ministers through the gifts He distributes among the people to minister, care for, and serve others.

Home Plate/Intimacy/Deep Fellowship

This brings us to home plate, intimacy, community, koinonia, the deeper uniting of the group members not only to one another, but also to Jesus Christ. And it is Jesus Christ who has made this unity possible by endowing the group with anointing "for the building up of the whole body."

In a sense, the facilitation of the group has shifted from an outside control to a wonderful new control system where the Spirit is free to move in and through the members of the group.

When you reach this point in a group process, you will know it. And until you have experienced it, there is no way to explain it. This is "group!" This is what it is all about, this is true *koinonia*, true "community."

How deep you go in community will be determined by how deep the people in the group want to go, and sometimes by how deep the culture allows.

Authentic Community Is Not Easy

The fact is that being faithful to the time it takes to become like family is not easy. According to Henri Nouwen, it is hard work. In *Can You Drink This Cup?*[2] Henri ventures into a very mystical and yet practical realm of realizing that when Jesus asks His friends James and John, the sons of Zebedee, *"Can you drink this cup?"* that it goes to the heart of our humanity as we must choose to hold, lift and drink to celebrate being fully human. This is the process of community, getting the whole cup from each other and drinking it.

There Are Some Serious Ways to See How Relations Develop[3]

Interpersonal relationships are *dynamic systems* that change continuously during their existence. Like living organisms, relationships have a beginning, a lifespan, and an end. They tend to grow and improve gradually, as people get to know each other and become closer emotionally, or they gradually deteriorate as people drift apart and form new relationships with others:

- *Acquaintance*—Becoming acquainted depends on previous relationships, physical *proximity*, first impressions, and a variety of other factors. If two people begin to like each other, continued interactions may lead to the next stage, but acquaintance can continue indefinitely.

- *Buildup*—During this stage, people begin to *trust* and care about each other. The need for compatibility and such filtering agents as common background and goals will influence whether interaction continues.

- *Continuation*—This stage follows a mutual *commitment* to a long-term friendship, romantic relationship, or marriage. It is generally a long, relatively stable period. Nevertheless, continued growth and development will occur during this time. Mutual trust is important for sustaining the relationship.

- *Deterioration*—Not all relationships deteriorate, but those that do, tend to show signs of trouble. Boredom, resentment, and dissatisfaction may occur, and individuals may communicate less and avoid *self-disclosure*. Loss of trust and betrayals may take place as the downward spiral continues.

- *Termination*—The final stage marks the end of the relationship, either by death in the case of a healthy relationship, or by separation.

Clear Communication Is Developed

I don't know who came up with the number five when it refers to communication, but everything I have ever studied over years gets stuck at five levels. As I have taught interpersonal communication to leaders all over the world, and in many cultures, I have come up with my own variations of the five. Communication is not rocket science, but there seems to be some skills and some tools that can help you do it more effectively.

My Own Five Stages

1. *Cliches/courtesies*—"Good morning." "How are you?" "Have a nice day."

2. *Facts/figures*—"Do you think it will rain today?" "Hey, how about those Dodgers?"

3. *Opinions/ideas*—"I don't think the new employee can pull it off." "I" sure hope we can finish up settling this management dispute."

4. *Feelings/emotions*—"Man, the driver of that car really frightened me." "I am so tired of feeling anxious."

5. *Risks/realities*—"Can we chat for a minute outside, I am struggling with…" "Hey, could you pray for my marriage, things are really not well."

As we engage in personal interaction, we often neglect the power of how we say something, more than what we are trying to say. Paying attention to nonverbal expressions is critical for clear connection and clear communication. There are three major parts of face-to-face communication that we cannot forget. They are body language, voice tonality, and words.

- 55% of impact is determined by body language—postures, gestures, and eye contact.

- 38% by the tone of voice.

- 7% by the content or the words used in the *communication process.*[4]

More Skills

Because effective communication is so essential in the discipleship process, whether one-on-one before or after a group meeting, or even in the context of the group time itself, we can incorporate some simple things:

- *Repetition:* Repeat the message the person is making verbally.

- *Contradiction:* Contradict a message the individual is trying to convey.

- *Substitution:* Substitute for a verbal message. For example, a person's eyes can often convey a far more vivid message than words and often do.

- *Complementing:* Add to or complement a verbal message. A boss who pats a person on the back in addition to giving praise can increase the impact of the message.

- *Accenting:* Accent or underline a verbal message. Pounding the table, for example, can underline a message.[5]

One thing for sure, how deeply and how quickly or slowly the discipleship process or the small group goes into intimate fellowship has many factors. Some will be related to the mix of the group, even the ratio of men to women, and much will be related to how deep the group wants to go, how much risk taking they enjoy, even the cultural ethos of the group, and what will be accepted or not accepted, or even tolerated.

As a leader, you can't force it, require it, or mandate it. But you can encourage it, ask for it, and most of all, model it. Groups have stages or seasons when chaos outrules order, and often during those seasons there is more sharing and giving to each other than during those subtler, more serene, or peaceful periods of group life.

So don't be afraid when it seems like the storms are many and the quiet times are scarce. But also enjoy all of the times of the pure fellowship and friendship of one another as if a gift. Remember, that is why we call it "the present."

Groups grow, not as they grow in number, but as they grow in depth, as the conversation and the intimacy goes deeper. As the caring becomes more tangible, and the interrupting and question asking becomes more intentional, often both the tears and the laughter will also increase.

We are fighting major cultural issues here, but we must stay at it, we must grow into deep, honest, fellowships of the heart that create a chaordic atmosphere where we can experience what it means to have someone really walk with us. This only happens in groups where people are free to talk together through the issues of life.

Nate Larkin, the founder of The Samson Society,[6] talks about what is common to the men that form Samson Society meetings all over the country. These meetings are similar in some ways to AA meetings, but use a very clear and deliberate biblical path that lead these guys to a deep relationship with Christ and deeper relationships with each other.

Our culture, especially with men, has created a generation of guys (even in the church) who are alone, distant, broken, and driven. Nate in the Samuel Society Charters provides a list as traits of men that are natural cultural tendencies, most of which can only be addressed in the context of small groups, and usually groups of just men. These traits surround the realities or perceptions that men (at least Western men) are natural loners, wanderers, liars, judges and strongmen.

Because of these and other deep issues, small groups that help people grow tend to ask a lot of questions and can tend to go all over the place in the communication process. Sure, there is an information process that comes through reading, curriculum, and designed studies. And, I think there is an important place for classes, seminars, and schools in the overall developmental process of making disciples and particularly raising up leaders.

But there is nothing like the unique dynamic of disciple making and mutual mentoring that comes only as you live out the consistent process of open-ended questions that bring out lively interaction.

In the long run, this is what tends to make these chaordic groups so effective in providing such an incredible atmosphere for growing deep as a group and experiencing a corresponding deeper personal growth. Again, that's why we have a huge list of questions at the back of this book that can keep those discussions going and growing.

Even as your typical study of the Word becomes more about the teaching of the Word, requires a teacher or pastor, and is content driven, that discussion is limited. But in these smaller, chaordic, discovery groups, no one person is always leading, always lecturing. But when you do this as a group you can fully enjoy reading through a passage, discussing together what comes up, and make incredible discoveries out of the shared thoughts and insights of many.

This also shouts volumes to a generation who have too quickly paid for others to study and research for them, once again missing the power of the priesthood of all believers.

Endnotes

1. Lyman Coleman, *Encyclopedia of Serendipity* (Littleton, CO: Serendipity House, 1980), 25.

2. Henri Nouwen, *Can You Drink This Cup?* (Notre Dame, Indiana: Ave Maria Press, 2006), 22-24.

3. http://en.wikipedia.org/wiki/Interpersonal_relationship.

4. Mehrabian and Ferris, "Inference of Attitude from Nonverbal Communication in Two Channels," *The Journal of Counseling Psychology* 31 (1967), 248-252.

5. www.helpguide.org/mental/eg6_nonverbal_communication.html.

6. www.samsonsociety.org.

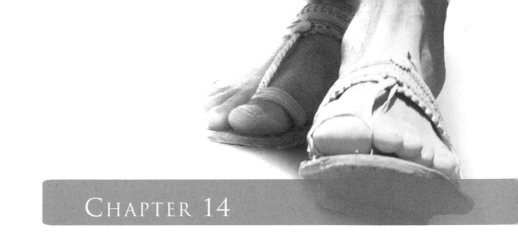

Chapter 14

Is Our Future Chaordic?

IN HIGH SCHOOL, I was a part of a track team that ran the 440 relays. My coach often said, sometimes the entire race comes down to one thing, the hand-off of the baton. As fast and as steady as a particular runner can run, if the baton isn't passed, and if not passed with relay-sync precision, it is not a relay team, but merely four separate runners trying to encourage the other guy ahead of him to run his part, and run it faster.

I personally think that the timing for rising up and releasing of the next generation of chaordic leaders to lead is one of the most critical realities of the future of the Church. My optimism of leading by mentoring and the impact of a mentoring model on an entire generation stimulates me. Of the many reasons that challenge me personally to lead differently, one of the major motivations is the fact that I must do a better job in passing along those values that grip me to those who follow me.

We are at a crossroads of leadership today. With the graying of the primary clergy from 48 to 53 since 1998, some pivotal decisions need to be made. In Abraham/Isaac, David/Solomon, Paul/Timothy moments, it is obvious that the survival of the next generation becomes more tantamount that the provision of the current one.

Those in the current positions of leadership must initiate this change for future generations. Namely, we who have led for the last 40-plus years must now have a plan to transition to the future generations of the Church.

I preserve in my memory a mental picture from a famous Bible story that involves two generations. Sometimes when I think of generations going together, I get this picture promise going in my head of David's return of God's box, the ark of the covenant, to the City of God. You may recall that David's first attempt at returning the ark on his newly crafted cart was a disaster, with David's friend Uzzah dying in his attempt to simply stabilize the vibrating cart over some unstable ground (see 2 Samuel 6).

But his second attempt shows the synergism of obedience and cooperation meant that two generations would carry God's manifest presence. It says in 1 Chronicles 15:14,15:

So the priests and the Levites sanctified themselves to bring up the ark of the Lord God of Israel. And the children of the Levites bore the ark of God on their shoulders, by its poles, as Moses had commanded according to the word of the Lord.

Much has been said about David's impetuous attempt at the transport of the ark on his newly designed wheels, and his need to repent and return to the designed means of moving the ark. The poles of the ark were meant to rest on the shoulders, the ark itself held high, above the minds of men, His presence and His ways, higher than ours. But what seems clear are one generation preparing the way for the other and the other generation following in that prepared way. Two generations together moving with God.

Three Generations

This possibility of two, maybe even three generations working together to carry this manifest presence of God may have its own set of challenges. As the son of a pastor and a father of a pastor, my latent optimism still hopes that someday generations could work together for the glory of God.

We are looking at possibly the most pivotal leadership demographic shift in all of history. Is it possible that maybe even three generations might overlap and cooperate in the mission of God in the world?

If we can learn to lead among these generations, each doing his or her part, we have a chance. But if we keep to the empire building that too often represents my generation, the Boomers, forget it. As one megachurch pastor noted, "I doubt if the next generation will even pay the light bill."

I know we need to pass on something new and radically different, much more than what feels like the handing over of the keys to a piece a real estate, or the transfer of a deed with property and equipment. And of course, this passing along of anything is assuming that a few of the Late Boomers (born 1956-1964), a few of the Generation X (1965-1976), and maybe even a few of the Millennials (1977-1990) will make a U-turn and find each other in camaraderie and commitment. And begin this by also embracing the seniors from the World War II demographics (1945 and earlier) and even the Mosaics (1990-present). An enormous cross-sectioned crowd could be ready to be radical disciples, together!

My generation seems to believe in the old ways of doing things, and if you can add any numeric success to the endeavors at all, the idea of prying that pulpit, that wireless microphone, and that Power-Point projector away from today's leader seems more difficult than prying away the light saber from Luke Skywalker.

To do this we may have to admit to the inevitable that for many, "the only baton the next generation will pick up is a dropped baton." Some may drop it in frustration. And others may drop it by leaving it. What we need is for leaders to pass it intentionally.

In my years of processing and dissecting what I want others around me to replicate, I have entered time and time again into what I have coined, "Talking new and acting old." This is what happens when you sit around with other leaders brainstorming how things could be done differently, confessing how different what is consistently done is from what was originally envisioned. Then, of course, as this late-night coffee-enhanced exercise is completed, you return to leadership and church as usual.

This twisted thinking that too quickly associates our methods with our mission has kept an entire generation of leaders in freeze-frame. I cannot tell you how much time I have spent talking about wanting to experiment with new leadership forms and methods, only to be prematurely rejected because we cannot separate what we do with why we do it.

This could be the biggest of hurdles. When the paradigm is completely different, it's often not possible to communicate between those paradigms. In those cases, older leaders are going to have to "drop the baton" and trust the Holy Spirit will move younger leaders to pick it up. They will simply run the same race, but in a completely new and different way.

We cannot ignore the conspicuous way the Scripture remains neither descriptive not prescriptive about how we do church. This keeps the door wide open for the constant shifts in methods and form. But in a culture that defines itself through empirical systems that demand repeating, any serendipitous or flexible way of leading is taboo.

In other words, the Scripture is clear that we are to lead. But how we lead, who we lead, what way we lead, how long we lead— all of this is to be led by this One whose mercies are new every morning and whose directions are new every moment.

The Law of Attraction

A new craze of our day is centered in a book about the Law of Attraction, and I now realize that for anyone to offer anything to someone else it must be accompanied by a desire from the person wanting to receive. This brings back the picture of a "person's gift making room for him." Let's suppose that to begin with you are walking with some in the next generation that actually want to be with you, they want what they see in you and may have even asked that you walk with them so that they can catch what you carry.

As I shared earlier when a younger brother asked if he could "shadow me," at the time I don't think I had full understanding or comprehension what that meant. Maybe I did not have a clue as to what that really entailed. I am better today about negotiating this type of relationship and what could happen. But it still means that someone wants what you have, and if you still live in a poverty spirit, you are not likely to give away what you think will not be replaced.

I like that picture of Jesus' friends who asked Him, *"Lord, teach us to pray"* (Luke 11:1). Jesus, rather than including prayer as part of His systematic approach to discipleship, or enclosing the subject in the curriculum He was printing up in the syllabus, simply prayed enough until they requested that He pass that thing called "prayer" along to them.

Sure, Jesus did many other things, and sure the disciples could have asked for tutoring in these other practices, we simply do not know that. Many believe that even the disciples could have figured out the connection of Jesus' early morning times in prayer with the Father (see Mark 1:35) and the power that flowed out of His life on a daily basis, however it was that they deduced the connection between prayer and a life of obedience and a life of power. And when they saw it, and discerned it, they wanted it, so then the request, *"Teach us to pray"* (Luke 11:1).

This begins to make even more sense in an interactive relational mentoring model. You get to be with the one you are mentoring long enough that they see things in you that cause them to make requests. One of my favorite definitions of evangelism has always been "loving people until they ask why." So the same principle fits here. Rather than random acts of kindness, or in this case, random acts of impartation, leaning on one another makes room for observation, and participation, which then demands and invites impartation.

I hope we are not so set in our tendencies toward what it is we feel people need to learn that our preprinted materials have to have a life of their own. We have spent too much of our lives determining what is valuable, not realizing that our prerehearsed homilies became ineffectual because they did not address the real and genuine "felt needs" of the individuals that we were trying to lead. It sadly became our ecclesiastical version of "read two verses and call me in the morning."

Things desperately have to change. To do this means we will have to abandon our "Top 10 Things Disciples Need to Know" and ask the harder questions. "Is my life attractive?" "Is it contagious?" "Are the truths I want to transfer to others actually timely as well as transferable?" And am I the kind of leader that "listens for," and "leads among?"

Will this generation pass along a new way of leading, a new place to lead from, and a whole new attitude positionally that feels more like Jesus, "the sheep man" leading, than the baton of leadership where we pass on principles of church growth and one-minute management?

Will we be willing to go down in history as a generation of coaches and mentors that ended up nameless and faceless, remembered only for their ability to have furthered their sons and daughters along into God-given destiny? Might we be known as a generation of leaders who led chaordically, not from our lofty towers of token discipling, but as leaders who really poured ourselves into this next generation and led among them and for them.

CHAPTER 15

DISCOVERY QUESTIONS
FOR LEADING SMALL GROUPS

AS ALWAYS, THE PURPOSE of these small groups is a lot of talk, a lot of chitchat, a lot of noise, a lot of interaction, a lot of chatter. So they don't turn into lectures in a living room, using short discovery-type questions can keep a group going and flowing. Pick two or three for a night, randomly, or even create your own cohesive series. As you use them and listen for the answers, you are also modeling that what the members of the groups and not just the leader have to say is important.

There will be nights when these questions aren't necessary, so don't use them. And even though some people will complain at the trivia of these questions, when asked and given opportunities for response, even the complainers still enjoy the outcome.

By the way, these are great question starters for one-on-one discipleship, as well. Sometimes they help in getting conversations going in the early stages of relationship.

❑ 1. Whom do you admire the most? In what ways does that person inspire you?

❑ 2. If at birth you could select the profession your child would eventually pursue, would you do so?

❑ 3. Do you feel ill at ease going alone to either a movie or dinner? What about the way you are now living?

❑ 4. If you knew that in one year, you would die suddenly, would you change anything about the way you are now living?

❑ 5. Would you like to be famous? In what way?

❑ 6. What do you strive for the most in your life: accomplishment, security, love, power, excitement, knowledge, or something else?

❑ 7. You are invited to a party that will be attended by many fascinating people you've never met. Would you go if you had to go by yourself?

❑ 8. If you were given the ability to project yourself into the past, but not return, would you do so? Where would you go and what would you try to accomplish if you knew you might change the course of history?

❑ 9. Would you be willing to make a substantial sacrifice to have any of the following: your picture on a postage stamp, your statue in a park, a college named after you, a Nobel Prize, or a national holiday in your honor?

❑ 10. How many of your friendships have lasted more than ten years? Which of your current friends do you feel will still be important to you ten years from now?

❑ 11. If someone were to write a book about you, what do you think the title would be?

❑ 12. What things make your life complicated?

❑ 13. In one line, what is life all about?

❑ 14. If someone could give you anything in the world for your birthday, what would you like it to be?

❑ 15. Of all the material possessions you have, what gives you the most pleasure?

❑ 16. Give three words to describe how you feel right now.

❑ 17. If you could hang a motto or saying in every home in the world, what would it be?

❑ 18. Share something that you fear.

❑ 19. What feelings do you have the most trouble expressing?

❑ 20. What one quality do you look for most in friends?

❑ 21. What activity do you engage in that involves all of you—your thoughts and feelings, your body and your spirit?

❑ 22. When was the last time you cried? Why did you cry?

❑ 23. Describe the "ideal wife."

❑ 24. What four things are most important in your life?

❑ 25. If you wrote a book today, what would the title be?

❑ 26. If you received $5,000 as a gift on the condition that you spend it quickly, how would you spend it?

❑ 27. Share one of the happiest days of your life.

❑ 28. What is something that makes you angry?

❑ 29. What do you want to be doing in ten years?

❑ 30. What is your favorite song?

❑ 31. Describe your life at age 70.

❑ 32. What do you like most about yourself?

❑ 33. Share a big let down in your life.

❑ 34. Thinking back, identify a turning point in your life?

❑ 35. What bit of advice would you give a young man about to get married?

❑ 36. Complete the statement, "A new world opened up to me when…"

❑ 37. Describe the "ideal husband."

❑ 38. Share a time in your life when you were embarrassed.

❑ 39. Do you ever feel lonely? When?

❑ 40. Complete the statement, "If I could live my life over again…"

❑   41.   Complete the statement, "One thing I missed during my childhood was…"

❑   42.   In what ways do you act like a child?

❑   43.   Share a frightening moment.

❑   44.   If you could live anyplace in the world, where would it be? Why?

❑   45.   What do you like to do in your spare time?

❑   46.   What is something that makes you feel sad?

❑   47.   What is something that really "bugs" you?

❑   48.   What do you dislike most about yourself?

❑   49.   What do like most about where you live?

❑   50.   Share a time when your feelings were hurt.

❑   51.   What talents do you have? (Don't be modest, be honest!)

❑   52.   What lifetime dream are you still trying to make come true?

❑   53.   What talent do you wish you had?

❑   54.   If you could receive a sixth sense, what would you want it to be?

❑   55.   If you could receive any spiritual gift, what would you want it to be?

❑   56.   When do you feel closest to God?

❑ 57. *"Jesus wept."* (Luke 19:41 & John 11:35) What makes you feel like weeping?

❑ 58. What is prayer to you?

❑ 59. What is your favorite hymn or worship song?

❑ 60. What song would you like sung at your funeral?

❑ 61. What is your favorite Bible story, and why?

❑ 62. What is your favorite name for God?

❑ 63. What epitaph do you want on your tombstone?

❑ 64. Jesus changed Simon's name to Peter, meaning "the rock" (see John 1:42) If Jesus changed your name what do you think your new name would be?

❑ 65. Describe "hell."

❑ 66. Describe "Heaven."

❑ 67. If you believe in God, what do you base your belief on?

❑ 68. What is your definition of sin?

❑ 69. Share a phrase that comforts you.

❑ 70. Share an experience of answered prayer.

❑ 71. What do you think it means to be "made in the image of God?"

❑ 72. What does this mean to you to: *"Bear one another's burdens?"* (Gal. 6:2)

❏ 73. Say something about your funeral.

❏ 74. In what ways does your faith in God affect your life?

❏ 75. What does "faith" mean to you?

❏ 76. What does "worship" mean to you?

❏ 77. What is your definition of a Christian?

❏ 78. What is something that you think God wants you to do?

❏ 79. What are three things that you believe about God?

❏ 80. What do you think your purpose in life is?

❏ 81. How do you tune into God?

❏ 82. If you were asked to preach a sermon, what would the title be?

❏ 83. What is the "Good News" according to you?

❏ 84. Share a personal spiritual experience that has built your faith.

❏ 85. How can one know God's will for his/her life?

❏ 86. Share a time when you believe God led you.

❏ 87. What character in the Bible do you relate to?

❏ 88. If you met Jesus face to face, what question would you like to ask Him?

❏ 89. What kind of animal would you like to be and where would you like to live?

❑ 90. Describe the "ideal mother."

❑ 91. Where would you like to go for a vacation if you could go anyplace in the world?

❑ 92. What does America mean to you?

❑ 93. What makes you feel frustrated?

❑ 94. When you are alone and no one can see you or hear you, what do you like to do?

❑ 95. What really turns you off?

❑ 96. Share three things for which you are thankful.

❑ 97. If you became president of the United States, what two things would you do?

❑ 98. Finish the sentence, "The best thing about today is…"

❑ 99. Describe the "ideal father."

❑ 100. What makes you laugh?

❑ 101. Tell what makes a happy family.

❑ 102. What kind of TV commercial would you like to make?

❑ 103. What would you like to become famous for doing?

❑ 104. What kind of store would you like to own and operate?

❑ 105. What would you do if you had an incurable disease?

❑ 106. Describe a "good neighbor."

❑ 107. What would you do if you found $1,000 in a vacant lot?

❑ 108. If you could change your age, what age would you rather be?

❑ 109. Where is your favorite place to be quiet and still? Why?

❑ 110. Tell about a time when you felt proud of yourself.

❑ 111. How do you look when you get angry?

❑ 112. What do you like to daydream about?

❑ 113. How would you describe yourself to someone who does not know you?

❑ 114. What do you think it's like after you die?

❑ 115. What color do you think of when you think of happiness?

❑ 116. If you could have been someone in history, who would you have been?

❑ 117. What is the worst thing parents can do to children?

❑ 118. How do you feel about growing old?

❑ 119. What is one of your hobbies?

❑ 120. How do you feel when someone laughs at you?

❏ 121. Name two famous people you'd like to have for parents.

❏ 122. What do you think about when you can't fall asleep?

❏ 123. What gives you "goose bumps?"

❏ 124. What would you like to invent to make life better?

❏ 125. If you were a doctor, what ailment would you like to cure?

❏ 126. What is something you can do pretty well?

❏ 127. If you could become invisible, where would you like to go?

❏ 128. What would you most like to do, or be, for the next five years if there were no limitations of family, money, education, health, etc.?

❏ 129. What would you do if you knew you couldn't fail?

❏ 130. Who is the most authentic (genuine) person you have met?

❏ 131. What is your most satisfying accomplishment? Ever? Before you were 6? Between the ages of 6 and 12? Between the ages of 12 and 18? After you turned 25?

❏ 132. Tell your strongest points (name three). Name your weakest points (three).

❏ 133. What is your happiest memory? (At various ages)

❏ 134. Describe the most significant event in your life.

❑ 135. Describe the characteristics of the "ideal" woman, or the "ideal" man.

❑ 136. What person(s) besides your parents has/have been the most influential in your life?

❑ 137. What present would you like to receive?

❑ 138. Whose approval do you need the most?

❑ 139. In whose presence are you the most comfortable? Why?

❑ 140. If you had what you really wanted in life, what would you have?

❑ 141. List your long-range goals…your short-range goals.

❑ 142. Describe the most excitingly creative person you have known.

❑ 143. List some creative ways to begin and to end a day.

❑ 144. What do you pray about most often?

❑ 145. What do you most trust in?

❑ 146. Who has changed your life?

❑ 147. Where would you live if you could, and what would you do there?

❑ 148. Tell who you are, apart from your titles, honors, or your job description.

❑ 149. What kind of social gathering do you like best?

❑ 150. What is the best book (apart from the Bible) you have ever read?

❑ 151. Describe your favorite way of spending spare time.

❑ 152. What feelings do you have trouble expressing or controlling?

❑ 153. What makes you feel depressed or blue?

❑ 154. What makes you anxious, worried, or afraid?

❑ 155. What gives you self-respect?

❑ 156. Describe the person who has meant most in your life other than a parent or a child. What are that person's outstanding characteristics?

❑ 157. Who was the first person you felt that really understood you?

❑ 158. Are you the kind of person others confide in? Why?

❑ 159. What kind of person do you confide in?

❑ 160. What makes a person a good listener?

❑ 161. What kind of listener do you think you have been in this group?

❑ 162. How do you feel this group has listened to you, both corporately and separately?

❑ 163. What makes a "good" marriage?

❑ 164. What would you like most to do in history?

❑ 165. What is your ideal for the future of society, both immediate and long range?

❑ 166. How could you help to change an injustice of which you are aware?

❑ 167. What is your middle name and how did you get it?

❑ 168. What was your favorite summer thing to do at age ten?

❑ 169. What is the best job you've ever had?

❑ 170. What is your most costly possession?

❑ 171. How do you spend your days off?

❑ 172. What is your favorite part of the circus?

❑ 173. What holiday most inspires you?

❑ 174. Concerning the remote, are you more likely to hog or share it?

❑ 175. For your birthday, do you prefer lots of presents or no presents?

❑ 176. What is your favorite food?

❑ 177. What is your least favorite food?

❑ 178. What is the favorite meal you have ever had?

❑ 179. What was the high point of this week? The low point?

❑ 180. What is your favorite place in the house, and why?

❑ 181. What is one job you enjoy doing around the house?

❑ 182. What hobby did you enjoy in your teens?

❑ 183. What is your nickname? When did you get it?

❑ 184. What was your first job?

❑ 185. What is the worst storm disaster you have ever been in?

❑ 186. What is the funniest thing that ever happened in a religious setting?

❑ 187. What is your favorite thing to do on a rainy day?

❑ 188. What is your most prized childhood possession, and why?

❑ 189. What is the best costume you've worn to a costume party or Halloween?

❑ 190. What was the most disastrous meal you've ever eaten or made?

❑ 191. Describe your first blind date. What happened?

❑ 192. What was your worst home decorating/fix-it experience?

❑ 193. Who was your weirdest neighbor? Why?

❑ 194. What was your hometown like?

❑ 195. If you like your pet, why?

❑ 196. What was your favorite teenage hangout?

❑ 197. What was your first car like?

❑ 198. Describe a time when "nature couldn't wait."

❑ 199. When is the first time you remember winning at something, and how did it make you feel?

❑ 200. If you could pick one character in fiction, TV, or even the comics to identify with, who would that be, and why?

❑ 201. What was the wildest prank you were ever involved in?

❑ 202. I am most like my mom in that I...?

❑ 203. Do you like your name? If you could choose another name what would it be?

❑ 204. If you could do any job you wanted to, what would you be doing five years from now?

❑ 205. What is the best advice you have ever received?

❑ 206. What makes a home a home?

❑ 207. Are there days you would like to be wallpaper? What would you do?

❑ 208. Who is the most famous person you've ever met? How did it happen?

❑ 209. What would you have been voted, "Most likely to" while in high school?

❑ 210. Describe the circumstances around your first kiss.

❑ 211. You can raise one person from the dead. Who? Why?

❑ 212. How did you get your nickname?

❑ 213. What is your greatest accomplishment?

❑ 214. What do you think is the perfect age? Why?

❑ 215. Describe the most unforgettable person you have ever met.

❑ 216. What song reminds you of an incident in your life?

❑ 217. What place that you visited would you never visit again?

❑ 218. Are you rushed for time in your daily schedule?

❑ 219. What things do you wish you could take out of your daily schedule?

❑ 220. If there were 25 hours in a day, what would you add to your daily schedule?

❑ 221. Your doctor says, "Slow down!" How are you going to adjust your daily schedule?

❑ 222. What is not in your daily schedule that needs to be?

❑ 223. What activities in your day constitute the most valuable use of your time?

❑ 224. What do you like most about yourself?

❑ 225. What one blessing have you received from this group?

❑ 226. Has there been a situation recently where you were instrumental in the growth of another person? What did you do?

❑ 227. If you could instantly make your job or marriage or church or family perfect, how would it be different than it is now? What is one thing you could do this week to move toward those changes?

❑ 228. What do you need to make your Christian life more meaningful and effective?

❑ 229. If you could live a year of your life over again, which year would you choose?

❑ 230. If you had to describe one frustration you've had with this group, what is it?

❑ 231. If given a choice, how would you choose to die?

❑ 232. If you were to describe yourself as a flavor, what would your flavor be?

❑ 233. Where do you go or what do you do when life gets too heavy? Why?

❑ 234. For what in your life are you the most grateful?

❑ 235. What was your most embarrassing moment?

❑ 236. Share a memory of your grandmother or grandfather.

❑ 237. What qualities do you prize most in a friend?

❑ 238. In what way are you different from the way people usually see you?

❑ 239. If you knew you could not fail, what two things would you try?

❑ 240. When was the first time you heard about Jesus? What did you think about Him?

❑ 241. When, if ever, did God become more than just a word to you?

❑ 242. When did you fully realize that your sins had been forgiven because of what Christ did for you?

❑ 243. What three things do you like/dislike about your father?

❑ 244. I am most like my father when I...?

❑ 245. What three things do you like/dislike about your mother?

❑ 246. What two things do you like about your appearance?

❑ 247. What do you do to take care of your health?

❑ 248. At work, what are you good at? Name two things.

❑ 249. What name do you use for God when you are intimately talking to Him?

❑ 250. Describe what you think "Heaven on earth" would be like.

About Gary Goodell

A former pastor, dean and Bible college instructor, Gary has been doing ministry stuff for over 40 years. He is a father of two married children and grandfather of six.

His son, Brian, Brian's wife, Cynthia, and their five children (Victoria, Keaton, Maxwell, Savannah, and Jackson) live in Foster City, California, where Brian leads a local fellowship in San Mateo, called "The Bridge."

His daughter, Becky, her husband, Enrique, and their daughter Sofia, live in Lake Forest, California. Becky and Enrique are both psychiatric technicians at Fairview Hospital in nearby Costa Mesa, and Enrique recently graduated from Vanguard University.

Co-author with Graham Cooke of *Permission Granted to Do Church Differently in the 21st Century*, Gary founded Third Day Churches in 2001 and is an itinerate coach and mentor for church planters and leaders in 15 nations. He and his wife, Jane, live in San Diego, California.

For more information please write:

Third Day Churches
P.O. Box 7531
San Diego, California USA 92167

Or visit:

www.thirddaychurches.com

Additional copies of this book and other book titles from DESTINY IMAGE are available at your local bookstore.

Call toll-free: 1-800-722-6774.

Send a request for a catalog to:

Destiny Image® Publishers, Inc.

P.O. Box 310
Shippensburg, PA 17257-0310

*"Speaking to the Purposes of God for This
Generation and for the Generations to Come."*

For a complete list of our titles,
visit us at www.destinyimage.com.